CW01655670

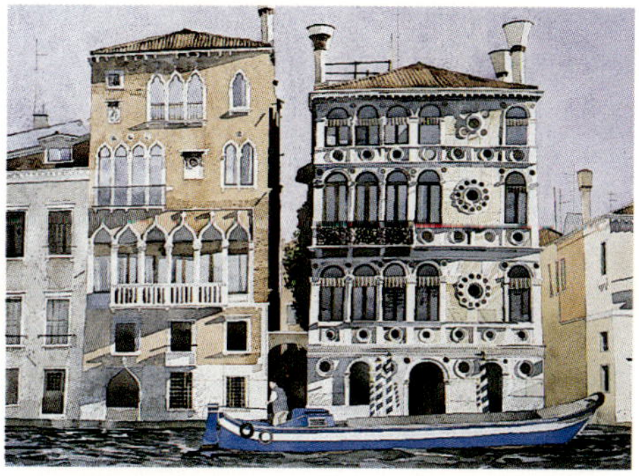

WATERCOLOUR

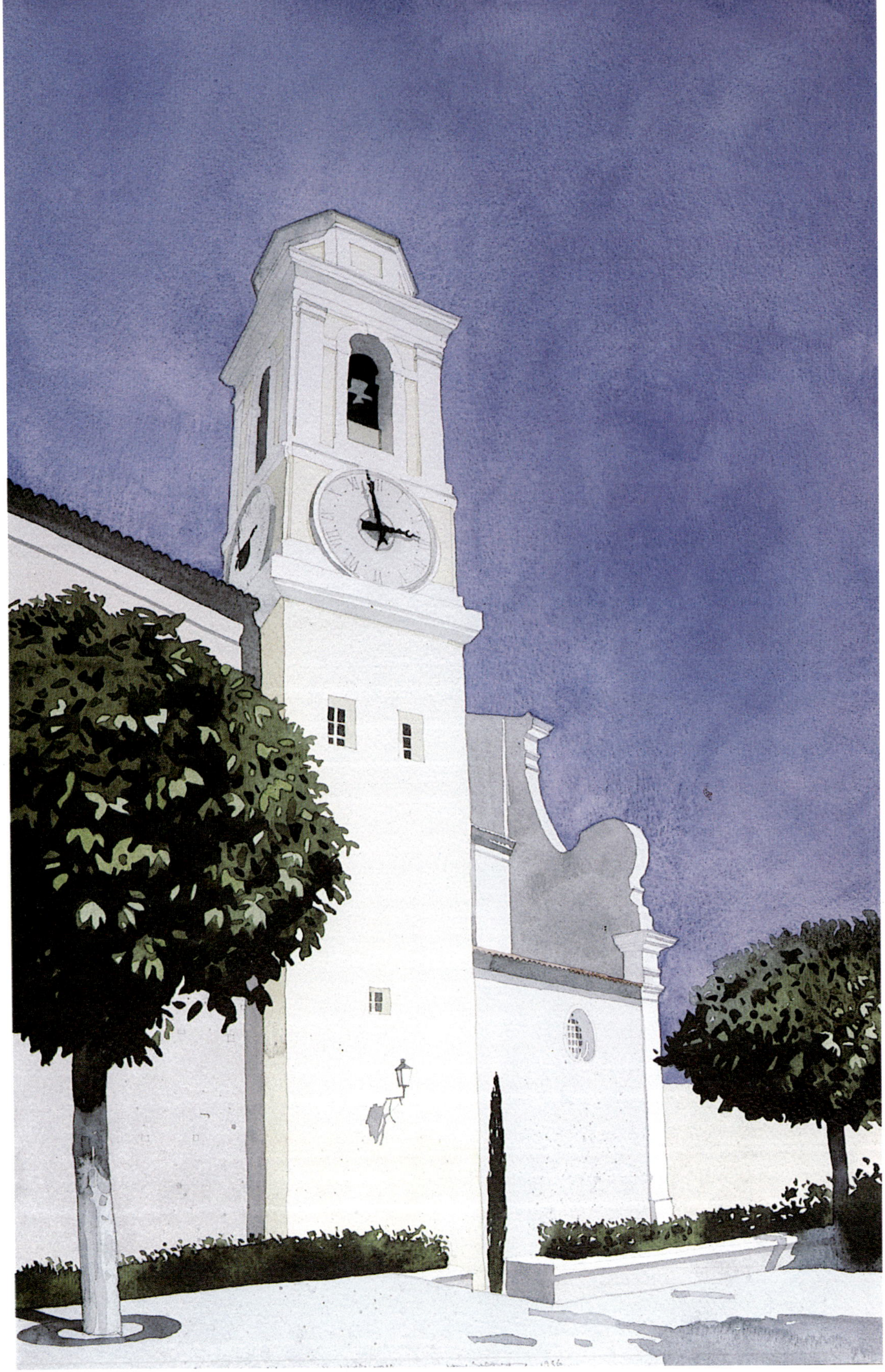

SUNBURST ART SERIES

WATERCOLOUR

Ian Sidaway

SUNBURST BOOKS

This edition first published in 1996 by
Sunburst Books,
Kiln House,
210 New Kings Road,
London SW6 4NZ

© Sunburst Books 1996

The right of Ian Sidaway to be identified as the author of this work has been asserted by him in accordance with the Copyright, Designs and Patents Act 1988.

All right reserved. No part of this publication may be reproduced, stored in a retrieval system, or transmitted in any form or by any means, electronic, mechanical, photocopying, recording, or otherwise, without the prior written permission of the publisher and copyright holders.

ISBN 1 85778 216 X

Printed and bound in China

CONTENTS

INTRODUCTION

WATER-BASED MEDIUMS have been in use for over twenty thousand years. Primitive watercolours, using paint made from ground pigments suspended in water and bound with animal fats, still survive in remarkable condition preserved on the walls of deep caves throughout Europe, protected as they are from changes in the atmosphere and the harsh light of day. A tradition had begun that would gain artistic strength throughout the three thousand years of the great Egyptian dynasties and increase in momentum with the creation of illuminated biblical text and manuscripts, which played such an important part in the birth of Christianity and the spread of the gospels throughout Europe during the Middle Ages.

Far across the world in China the watercolour tradition had developed independently into an essential skill. It was considered to be a spiritually uplifting and meditative pastime practised by all learned folk, and it is perhaps here that the true beginnings of watercolour, as we know and use the medium today, began. The Chinese artists exploited the white of the paper, which they invented around one hundred years before the birth of Christ, and they made use of transparent washes of colour and tone. Both of these techniques are still central to the traditional method of watercolour painting.

In Europe throughout the 15th, 16th and 17th centuries watercolour was used by relatively few artists, and it was not until the end of the 18th century that the potential of this medium began to be fully explored and exploited by a group of English landscape painters. It was an age of enlightenment and the obligatory European grand tour, and there was a steady demand for books and prints that included paintings or engravings of archaeological, historical and topographical scenes. The landscape as subject, as the Chinese so readily acknowledged centuries before, is well suited to the watercolour treatment, and the artists of the time, professional and amateur, experimented hard, looking for and developing satisfactory techniques to convincingly depict the ever changing light and effects of the weather. In doing so, watercolour finally came of age. Little wonder it was thought of as the English medium.

There is little doubt that watercolour holds a very special appeal and fascination. Perhaps it is that so much can be accomplished with so little or perhaps it is because many watercolours look deceptively simple, spontaneous and effective, and the results so achievable and quick to accomplish. In reality, successful results come quickly only occasionally. More often than not the painting has taken a great deal of planning and forethought, and there lies the key to success.

Despite watercolour's unpredictability, which for many is part of its attraction, by thinking logically, working methodically and with a little perseverance and practice, success will surely follow. It is also important to remain flexible and to be ready to make the most of those chance effects that are an inherent part of the medium. Do not be dissuaded by the first inevitable failures. Try a new tack, a different paper or brush and things will begin to click; suddenly a wash will go down flat and colours begin to run together in just the right way. But be warned; watercolour is a seductive medium and you may, given time, find yourself becoming involved in a serious love affair.

How to use this book

This book serves as an introduction to some of the many basic techniques that are in common practice. After the chapter dealing with materials and equipment, you will find a chapter that shows the techniques used throughout the book. It is my belief that practising, experimenting and becoming familiar with these techniques, without painting a picture, will help give confidence in handling the materials. The projects gain in complexity, each one combining a range of techniques with specific picture-making principles. You will be shown how to lay and combine washes, how to mask out areas to prevent them being covered in paint, how to use the white of the paper and how to create a range of textural effects, to name but a few. You will also be shown alternative paintings that deal with and solve similar problems to those illustrated in the project paintings. While you work, remember that painting is a subjective process; while there are certain principles that need to be acknowledged these are always open to wide and varied interpretation, and it is the interpretation that makes for artistic individuality.

MATERIALS AND EQUIPMENT

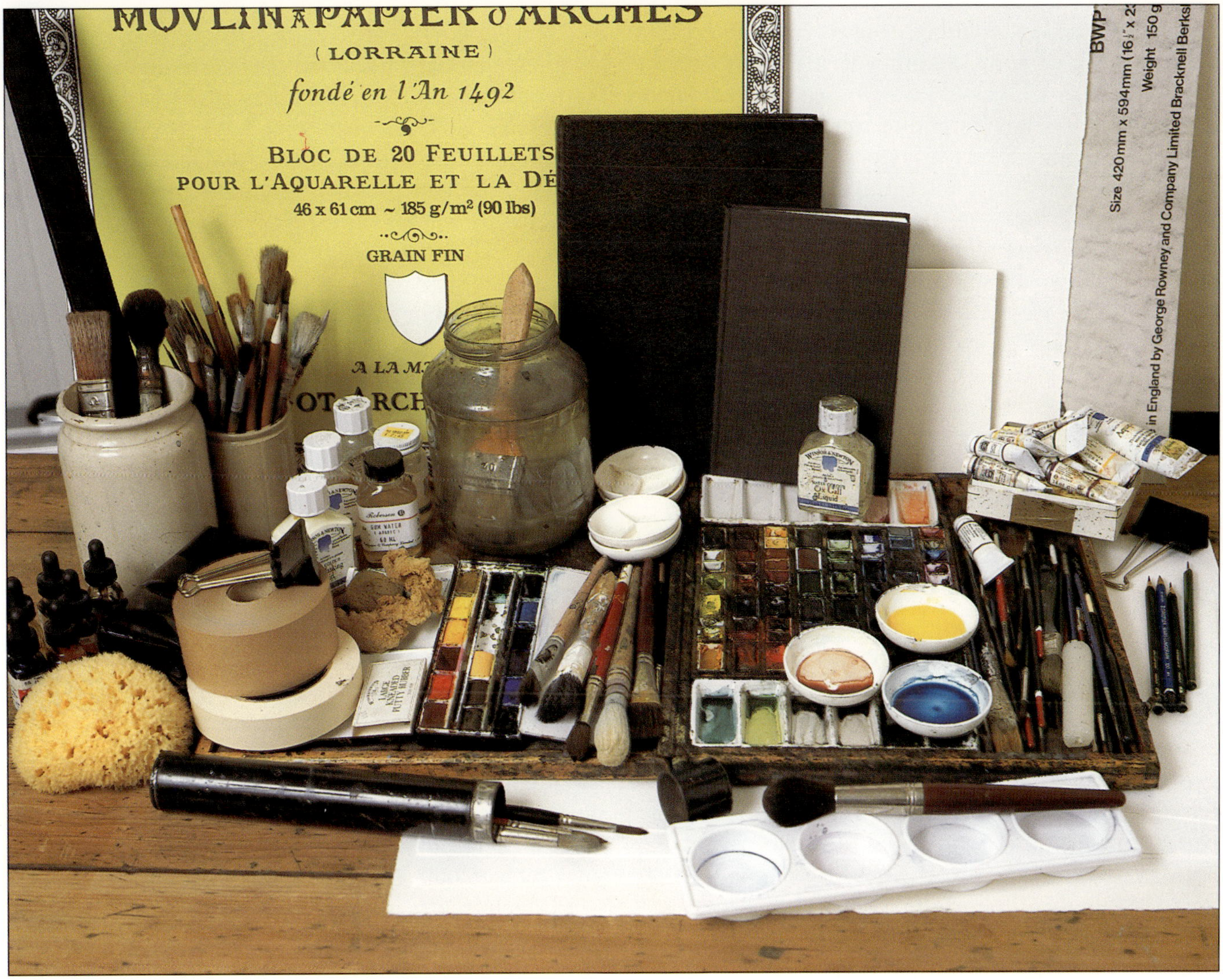

THE TRADITIONAL SUPPORT for watercolour painting is white or pale off-white paper. For the watercolourist the support is of primary importance: it is the brilliance and texture of the paper, combined with the transparent painted washes, that give watercolour paintings their inner light and freshness.

Types of paper and board

The various types of paper have very marked characteristics that make them behave in different ways – some are easy to use and very forgiving, while others can be awkward. With experience artists hit on one or two papers that suit their subject matter and way of working. Finding the right paper can be a matter of trial and error, but hitting on a difficult paper at the start could put the beginner off watercolour painting.

Papers come in a wide range of size, texture and weight, and most papers are sized with gelatine to give a surface that readily accepts the paint. Size can be added to the paper during manufacture, either at the pulp stage (internal sizing), or applied to the surface of the sheet of paper after it has been made (external sizing). The more size a paper contains the easier it is to remove paint from its surface, which is very beneficial for first-time watercolourists.

Papers are either handmade or machine made: the best handmade papers are made from pure linen rag processed to remove all the impurities and sized on one side only, this being the correct side on which to work. They are usually watermarked or embossed with the manufacturer's name and have a ragged, or 'deckle', edge. Machine-made papers are manufactured from wood pulp and come with three types of surface: Hot Pressed paper, which is smooth with little or no surface texture; Not or CP (Cold Pressed) paper, which is not hot pressed and has a definite tooth or texture; and Rough, which has a very pronounced tooth.

All three surfaces offer a suitable surface for the watercolourist; however two out of the three have idiosyncrasies that can make them difficult and awkward to use. The smooth Hot Pressed papers are in many ways better suited to drawing, as paint tends to slide over the surface and work can look flat and tired, but flat washes take well and the smooth surface makes it a good choice for fine detail. Rough surface papers can be very rough indeed, making the paint difficult to control, but washes do lie well on the pitted surface, allowing the white of the paper to show through, which gives a satisfying sparkle to the work. Rough surface papers are often favoured by landscape artists. Not papers offer the most adaptable and forgiving surfaces on which to work; the slight tooth makes laying washes straightforward and the surface is smooth enough to take detail.

A paper's thickness is indicated by its weight: the heavier the weight the thicker the paper. Two systems exist for measuring weight: the first is in pounds, and refers to the weight of a ream (500 sheets) of that particular paper, for example, 140lb, 260lb; the second is in grams, and refers to the grams per square meter (gsm) of one sheet, for example, 300gsm, 356gsm.

Thick papers over 300lb (638gsm) can withstand heavy work. They stay flat when wet and resist cockling, so do not generally need stretching. Medium and lightweight papers below 300lb benefit from being stretched, although some of the medium-weight papers do stay relatively flat when worked on unstretched.

Paper can be bought in pads, in which the sheets of paper are glued together along all four edges so do not need stretching. When a painting is finished, the sheet can be cut from the rest on the pad, revealing a clean sheet of paper ready for work. Watercolour boards that are stable when wet and require no preparation are also available, but, unfortunately, they are only sold in a very limited range of surfaces.

Paints

The quality of watercolour paint varies greatly, and therefore – perhaps more than any other medium – it pays to buy the best that you can afford.

Watercolours are made from finely ground pigments mixed with distilled water, gum arabic, glycerine or honey to keep the paint moist and to act as a preservative. The cheaper, or student-quality, paints are often made with pigments that are less pure and have a filler added that extends the pigment, making the colours weaker and slightly chalky. Paints in the professional artists' colour range dissolve easily when wet and, for the most part, are permanent, strong and resistant to fading. The colour is strong yet transparent and, as already mentioned, it is the paint's tendency to lie on the paper in semi-transparent washes – allowing previous layers and the brilliant white of the paper to show through – that is central to successful watercolour painting.

Paint is available in semi-moist pans, half pans, tubes of moist colour and bottles of liquid-concentrated colour. The liquid colour comes in bottles complete with a dropper fitted in the top, so the colour can easily be transferred to the palette. These are ideal for working on large formats in the studio where big washes (washes using large amounts of paint) are needed. Unfortunately, liquid colours are not as easy to mix as the pan and tube colours. Liquid colours were originally formulated for illustrators and designers who used them for work intended for reproduction, and they tend not to be as light or as fast as the artist's pan and tube colours.

Tube colours are also useful when working on a large scale, where paints need to be diluted in large amounts. When mixing tube colour never squeeze it out of the tube directly into water, as this makes it difficult to mix thoroughly and difficult to gauge the colour. Always squeeze some onto a palette and use a brush to transfer small amounts to another palette containing water. In this way the strength of the mixture is built up until the desired colour or tone is achieved. Any dried, leftover paint can be reused by wetting in exactly the same way as you would use paint in pans. For this reason it makes sense to squeeze colour out onto the same palette or area of palette.

Pan colours are easy to use, and for the novice watercolourist they are the best, as their very nature forces the artist to take colour from the pan and mix it with water in a shallow dish or on the palette in relatively small amounts, making the mixing of tones and colour a more exact exercise. However, always remember that the colour will look duller and darker once the paint has dried. To this end, it is always good practice to keep a sheet of paper handy on which to test colours in their wet and dry states before using them.

When exposed to light over a period of time certain pigments are prone to change, with the result that the colour becomes lighter and eventually fades. These colours are known as 'fugitive'. Thankfully, because of improved methods of manufacture and the increasing use of synthetic pigments, there are now only a handful of colours that are considered fugitive: the majority are durable or permanent. Manufacturers' classifications for permanence, which is carried on each tube and pan wrapper, are: AA****, extremely permanent; A***, durable considered permanent; B**, moderately durable; and C* Fugitive. Those pigments that are difficult to manufacture or obtain are more expensive than others, so paint is sold either as a series numbered 1,2,3,4, or lettered A,B,C,D, to indicate the price structure; the higher the number or letter the more expensive the paint.

Watercolours are available as separate colours or in boxes containing as many as 24 colours. The range of colours are chosen by the manufacturers and some may not contain the most useful selection, so you may prefer to buy an empty, unfitted box and fill it with your own choice of colours. Whether you choose pans or tubes is really a personal choice, but bear in mind that when, and if, you are working outside all you need to do with pan colours is add the pigment to the water. There is no squeezing out of colours from tubes onto a palette, and pan colours make packing up easy and quick should the weather or the natives turn ugly. A range of plastic or black enamelled metal boxes are available. Some even contain a water bottle, water container and mixing palette, which makes them very portable, tidy and ideal for small paintings done away from the studio.

Brushes

Soft brushes suitable for watercolour painting are available in a wide range of shape, size and quality. They are made from either synthetic fibre, natural animal hair or a mixture of both. Different brushes serve very different purposes, so it is inevitable that you will find yourself accumulating several; the type and range you choose will depend very much on your subject matter and the manner in which you work. It is perfectly possible, however, to work successfully with as few as three different brushes that have been carefully chosen.

Sable brushes are by far the best: they are also the most expensive, as they are made from the tail hair of the red Siberian mink. The Kolinsky sables fill and hold liquid well, keep their point, shape and spring, and, if looked after, will last a lifetime, justifying their high initial cost. The larger wash brushes are made from the hair of a variety of animals including ox, pony, goat and squirrel. These are softer than the sable brushes and lack their springiness. It is also possible to buy a very good brush made from synthetic fibres mixed with natural sable, which will, to a lesser extent, match some of the qualities found in a more expensive brush. For a more moderate price, brushes made entirely from synthetic fibres also do a very good job; many artists use nothing else, but even if they are well looked after they will soon lose their shape and point and need replacing.

The most useful brushes for all-round use come in three main shapes: round, flat and mop. Because of their shape, 'rounds' can successfully cope with a range of jobs from laying down broad, flat washes to fine intricate detail, and are the best brush for all-round use. By varying the pressure and increasingly splaying out the hair, it is possible to achieve a wide range of line thickness. In normal circumstances, working on a modest scale, with just two of these brushes, a no 12 and a no 6, you should be able to deal with most eventualities. 'Flats' lay colour in a regular, chisel-shaped band according to the width of the brush. With practice you can use them on their side to make a thinner line, but their main strength lies in their capacity to lay even, controlled flat washes. 'Mops' are either round or slightly flattened, and, depending on their size, can hold huge quantities of paint, making them ideal for laying in the initial loose, overall washes and for working on a larger scale.

The other shapes of brush that you will inevitably come across serve rather more specific needs and purposes. These go by a variety of names: rigger, fan, hake and oriental. The rigger consists of long hairs and is designed specifically to hold plenty of paint for making long, straight or curved fine lines. The fan-shaped brush is a useful addition if you anticipate doing a lot of dry brushwork; it is also used for blending. The hake is a large, flat brush, available in widths up to 15 cm/6 in and usually made from goat hair. This brush is used for washes and the broad, one-stroke application of paint across large areas. The oriental brushes come from China and Japan and are made from a variety of natural hair including wolf, deer and horse. Held together and glued into a bamboo handle, they can take a little getting used to, as they are not designed for western-style painting. Many of the oriental techniques require the brush to be kept more or less in an upright position; however they do hold paint well, keep their points and are very versatile.

Brushes come in series and each series contains the same shape brush in different sizes. As a rule round brush sizes begin at 000, the smallest, and increase in size up to 12 or 14, the largest. Flat brush sizes are indicated by the width of the brush, beginning at 3 mm/⅛ in and running up to 50 mm/2 in or more depending on the series. Mops run 4,6,8,10,12, and oriental brushes come in the very sensible range of small, medium and large.

No brush, no matter what its cost, will last long and give of its best if it is not looked after. Follow these few simple rules to keep your brushes in good shape for a long time.

Never leave brushes resting on their points or ends in jars of water.

Always rinse the brush clean of paint after use, paying particular attention to any accumulations around the ferrule (the point at which the hairs join the handle), then shape up the hairs into a point, or, if the brush is a flat, make sure the hairs are together with no gaps showing.

Store the brush upright in a jar or suitable container with nothing touching the hair or bristles.

Finally, if the brushes are not going to be used for a long time, make sure they are completely dry and put them into an airtight container to prevent moth grubs from eating them.

Water, other additives and masking fluid

Some books suggest using only distilled water to dilute the paint, because the pigment particles will then be suspended evenly, as distilled water is free of salts and other impurities. Very hard or very soft water can also affect the colours and the way the paint takes to the surface of the paper. However, as a general rule, this is both unnecessary and impractical, so unless you experience any strange occurences when you apply your paint, use ordinary clean tap water; never use dirty river water or sea water. Working with clean water, which avoids contaminating your mixes, is always good practice. Try to get into the habit of using two jars of water – one for cleaning your brushes in, the other for mixing your colours – and remember to change them frequently.

Some heavily sized papers repel water that has a high surface tension, causing it to sit on the surface in little puddles rather than spreading evenly and soaking into the paper. This is known as cissing. By adding a wetting agent such as oxgall to your water, the surface tension is reduced, enabling the water to flow and lie flat and even on the paper's surface. Glycerine can also be added to your mix. This substance also acts as a wetting agent, and it will extend the drying time of the paint slightly, which can help if the weather or atmosphere is warm and you are working with large amounts of paint (big washes). Alcohol added to the paint has the opposite effect and speeds up the drying time.

Gum arabic and gum water, which is a thinner solution of gum arabic, thicken the paint and make brush marks keep their shape; the effect depends on how much is used. They also increase the brilliancy and transparency of the colours and the solubility of the dry paint, which means that washes laid over areas of paint with gum arabic or gum water added will partly dissolve those areas. For this reason, they are best added to the final stages of a painting rather than the first or initial washes. If too much gum is used the paint surface will be glossy, and with very heavy use the layer of colour can crack and peel off. Because watercolours dry lighter and duller, the addition of gum arabic or gum water can help retain the rich glow that is seen in the wet paint.

Watercolour medium – a mixture of gum arabic, acetic acid and water, which can be bought at art stores – serves a similar function. It also serves as a wetting agent and improves the flow of the paint. Aquapasto is a thick paste which, when added to the watercolour, gives it a thick, buttery consistency that holds the shape of any marks or textures made in it (impasto), making possible a range of effects. Similar results can be achieved by mixing watercolours with any of the water-based acrylic mediums available, but take care not to contaminate your pans of watercolours with any of these, as once dry they are no longer soluble and could therefore spoil your paints, making them unusable.

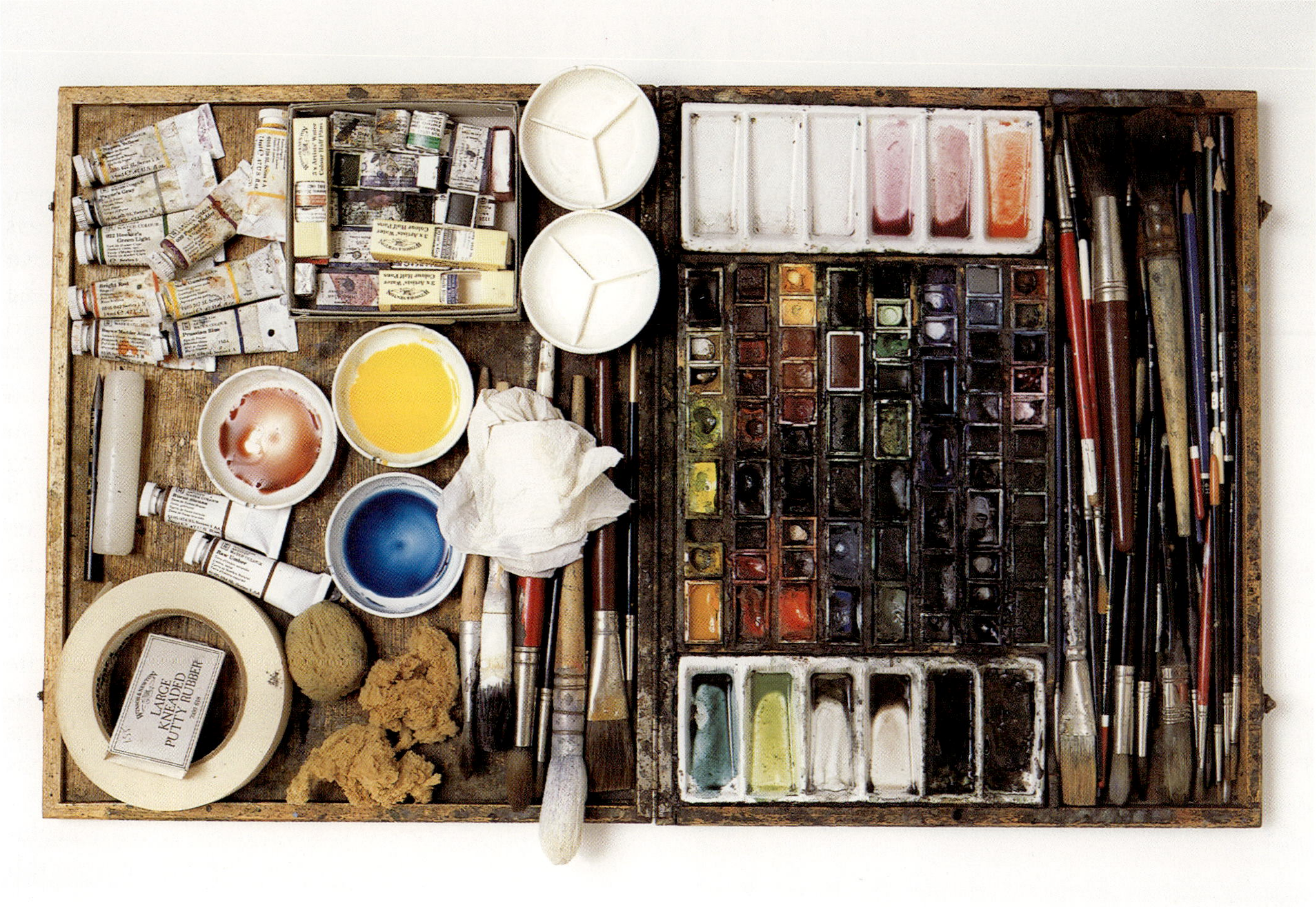

Masking fluid is not a medium or additive, but a liquid rubber solution that is applied by brush or pen directly from the bottle to mask out areas where paint is not required. It dries quickly and can easily be removed once the work is dry by gently rubbing the area with a finger; it is available in white or very pale yellow. Do not allow the fluid to stay on the paper for too long – it will become increasingly difficult to remove – and do not use your best brushes to apply the fluid, as they will very quickly be spoiled. Save an old brush or buy a cheaper one to be used just for the purpose. The fluid, when wet, can be washed from the brush with soap and water, or, if the fluid has dried, the brush can be rubbed with lighter fluid, which will dissolve the rubber.

Easels, palettes and sundry equipment

For watercolour work an easel is perhaps only really necessary if you are going to work outside, in which case you will need one that is not only lightweight and stable, but also enables your drawing board and paper to be positioned horizontally, so that the paint doesn't run and spoil your work. Indoor work can be done on a table with the board propped up at a slight angle with books; alternatively, use a table easel that is capable of being set at different angles. A drawing board or boards on which paper can be stretched can be bought at an art store, but you can very easily make a selection of various sized boards by cutting up a sheet of thick, medium-density fibre board. This will cost a fraction of the price of one proper drawing board and has the added advantage of enabling you to stretch several sheets of paper at one time.

Palettes with separate wells, or recesses, will prevent colours running together. Metal, ceramic and plastic types of various designs and layouts are readily obtainable. Some of the plastic types have larger wells and are perfect when mixing large quantities of dilute paint. Ceramic palettes tend not to hold quite so much paint, but are very easy to clean; many artists use ordinary dinner plates and saucers to mix their paints on. Never throw away a plastic yoghurt or cream pot, as they make perfect containers for mixing big washes in. Both natural and man-made sponges can be put to many a use – applying colour, making textures, lifting out colour to correct mistakes or to create highlights – as can cotton wool buds. Finally, a good supply of kitchen towels is invaluable for mopping up spills, blotting off excess paint and correcting those all too frequent mistakes.

TECHNIQUES

A GOOD AND SOUND knowledge of technique is perhaps more essential when using watercolour than with any other medium. Being able to successfully use and manipulate washes, knowing what will happen when wet paint is introduced onto a damp surface, when to add gum arabic into a mix in order to bump up the intensity of the colour, how to remove an area of paint and how to mask an area out and create a complicated edge are just a few of the many techniques that might need to be brought together at any one time, each playing their own crucial role in making a successful and satisfying painting.

Watercolour can be difficult to master; it is an unpredictable and often infuriating medium that can seem to have a mind of its own, yet taken individually many of the techniques are surprisingly simple and easy to do. But to gain confidence techniques need to be practised. Your approach needs to be focused and planned, while always remaining flexible and ready to seize upon a chance effect, watermark or run of paint – weaving them into your plan of things. Being able to recognise the potential of these chance happenings is a technique in itself, but one that, unlike the techniques that follow, cannot be taught.

The Techniques

▲ The laying and manipulation of transparent washes is the fundamental watercolour technique. Flat washes, where one consistent tone of colour covers a substantial area, are achieved by mixing up sufficient colour to complete the wash without running out. Slightly tilt the board on which you have stretched (see page 18) your paper, load a large brush – round or flat – with paint and, beginning at the top, make a steady horizontal stroke across the paper. The tilting of the board causes the excess paint to collect along the bottom edge of the stroke. Load the brush again and make another horizontal stroke slightly overlapping and just below the first. The excess paint now collects at the bottom of this stroke. Continue to overlap strokes working downwards until the area is covered. Run a semi-dry brush along the bottom to collect the excess paint and leave it to dry at the same angle. Many people find it easier to slightly dampen the paper surface first with a sponge and clean water.

▲ The graded wash is applied in the same way as a flat wash, but with each horizontal stroke either more water or pigment is added to the mix, depending on whether the wash is to become lighter or darker in tone. Be careful not to add too much water or pigment to each stroke, or the tonal jump between each one will be too noticeable. Variegated washes are similar, but rather than using just one colour, two or more are used side by side, the different colours blending into each other. The effects, while unpredictable, are good when painting dramatic skies.

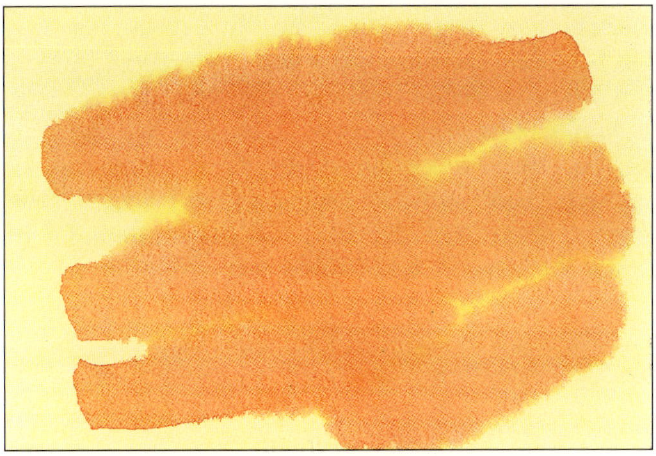

▲
When working wet into wet, paint is applied to an area that is already wet with paint or water. The freshly introduced paint bleeds into the wet surface and mixes on the paper, creating very seductive, soft blends of colour. The result is to a certain extent unpredictable and depends on how damp the paper surface is and the strength of the colour mix that is introduced. If the paper surface is wet, the colour blends quickly over a large area and is impossible to control. If, however, the surface is only damp, the bleed is smaller and slower and more easily positioned and manipulated. The resulting image will have no hard edges and will look blurred and amorphous.

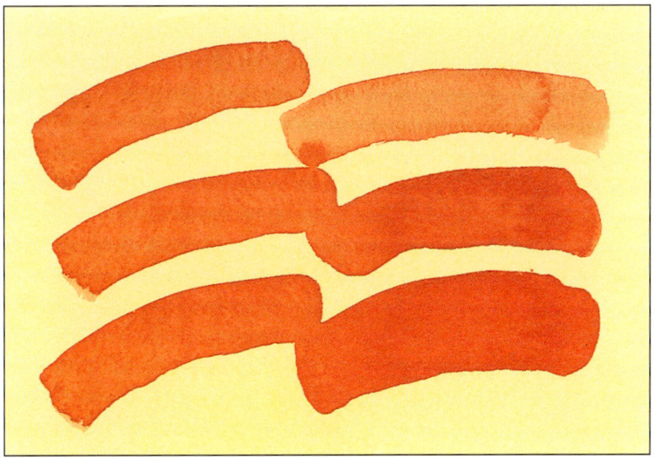

▲
Wet over dry is, as its name suggests, working wet washes over a dry surface and is used in tandem with wet-into-wet techniques to sharpen up the image and pull it into focus. Paint that is applied to a dry surface retains its edge, quality and shape, and stays where it is put; this allows detail to be added and colours modified without fear of them bleeding into one another. To obtain a crisp edge, the paint must be completely dry, and the judicious use of a hair dryer can hurry the process along.

▲
Certain coarse pigments used in watercolours have a habit of separating from each other, or granulting, when mixed with other pigments. As they dry they give a very fine, speckled texture. This can be used to good effect in shadows and when painting clouds and landscapes. Cobalt blue, ultramarine, manganese and cerulean blue, together with the earth colours yellow ochre, burnt sienna, burnt umber, raw sienna and raw umber all behave this way to a greater or lesser extent.

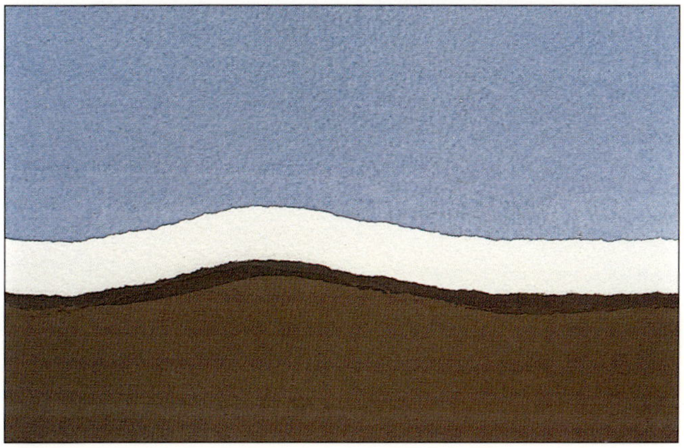

▲
Masking serves two purposes. First, it protects areas from being contaminated by unwanted paint and effects – for instance an area of work may be considered complete, but an adjoining area may need some vigorous spattering. By covering the finished portion of the painting no unwanted spots of colour will fall on it. The same principle applies if an area of white paper needs to be retained to serve as a highlight or, for example, a whitewashed building; by masking the area the paper will stay clean and free of paint. Second, the masking material serves to introduce a different edge or line quality into the work. Paper makes an ideal mask, as it can be cut to shape, creating a sharp edge, or torn. Paper will tear in a variety of ways depending on how thick it is, but it always gives an interesting edge; medium to heavyweight paper is better than thin paper for this purpose. Thin paper tends to cockle as it gets wet.

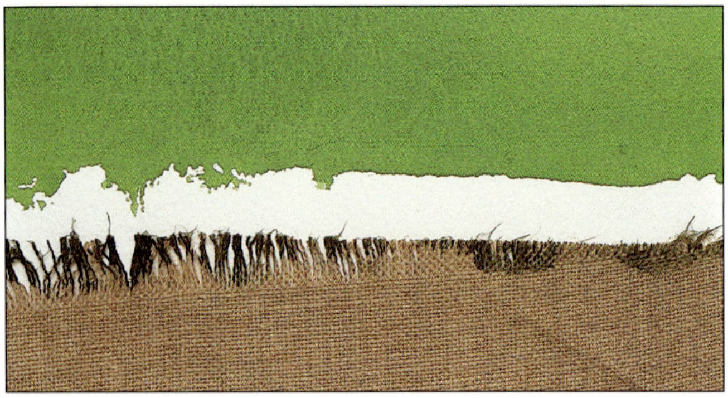

Fabrics can be used for masking and the coarser hessians and canvas are especially good, as the fibres along the edge unravel to make a broken line. You will need to work quickly because the paint will bleed under the mask as the fabric becomes wet; work away from the fabric so as not to push the paint under it. Wait until the paint dries before removing the mask carefully, or you run the risk of smearing the paint.

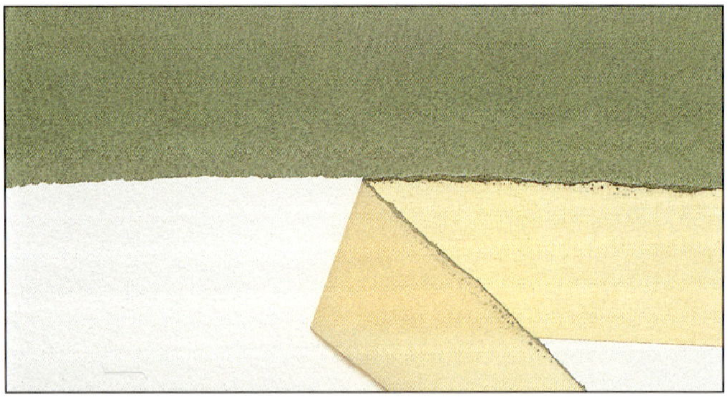

Masking tape comes in a variety of widths. The thinner widths can be used to create straight lines, while the wider tapes can be torn to create lines similar to those made with torn paper. Wider tapes may also be cut into intricate shapes with a scalpel. When applying the tape do not press it too firmly, and take care when peeling the tape off the paper not to pull and tear the surface.

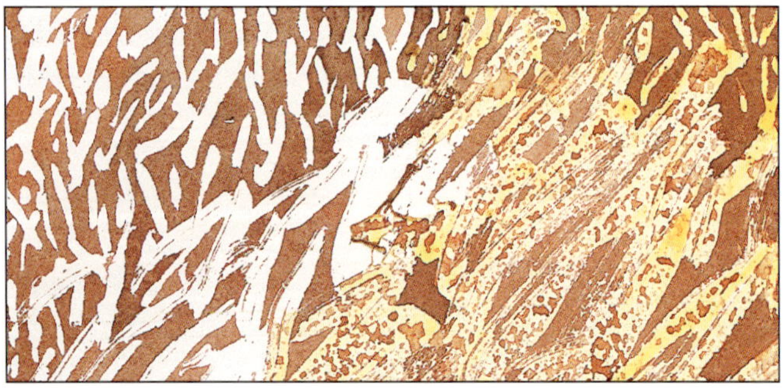

Masking fluid comes in two colours – yellow and white. The yellow is preferable, for the simple reason that it is easy to see against the white of the paper. It can be applied to the surface with a variety of brushes and dip pens; in fact any brush mark that can be made in paint can be made in masking fluid. When the solution is dry, forming a rubbery film, paint can be applied freely without danger of it colouring the covered area. Once the paint is dry the masking fluid can easily be removed by rubbing it with a finger.

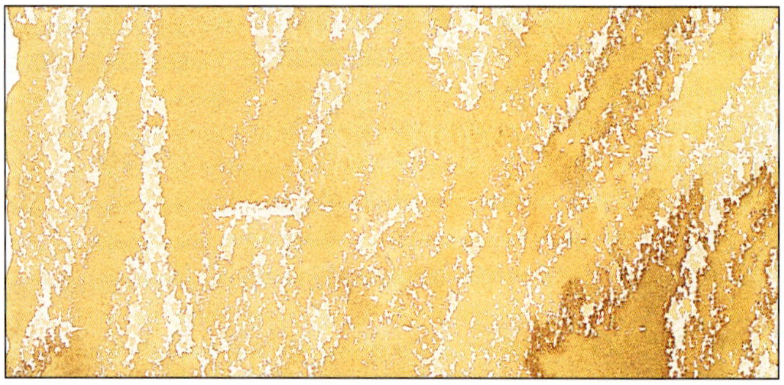

A white wax candle can be used to draw lightly onto the paper. The wax catches on the tooth of the paper, and when the area is painted the wax repels the paint, which then settles in those areas where there is no wax – leaving the white of the paper or, if applied over a painted area, the underlying colour showing through. This is ideal for brickwork or tree bark.

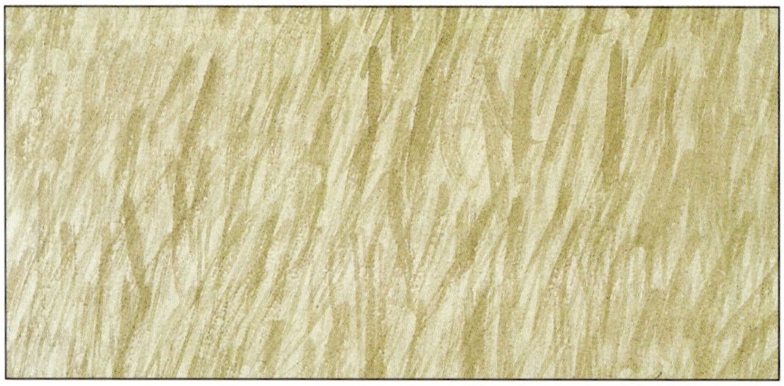

In dry brush work the excess paint is removed from the bristles, leaving them damp and containing a minimum of paint. The brush is then applied to the dry painting surface and the paint is pulled from the brush by the tooth of the paper. The paint can be removed from the brush by squeezing the brush between the fingers or touching it onto a piece of blotting paper. Alternatively, to apply the paint to the brush, mix up an amount of paint in a deep palette and soak a piece of screwed-up kitchen towel in it. The towel will soak up the paint, and if the brush is then pulled across the towel it will pick up just enough to make the mark. Use a flat brush or, if using a round one, splay the bristles between the thumb and finger.

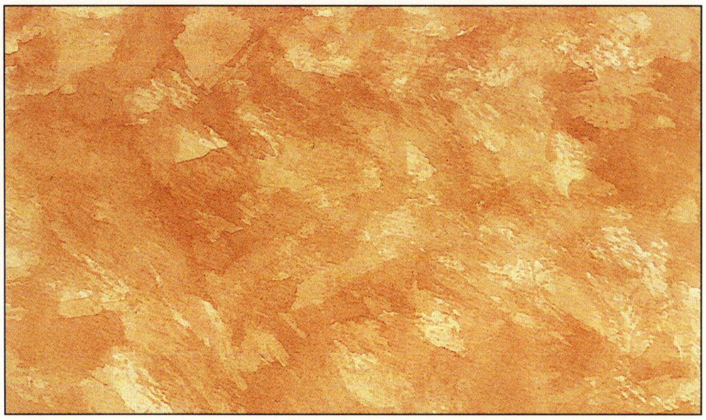

▲ As with the dry brush, paint applied by scumbling is not flooded onto the surface but scrubbed unevenly across the surface, thereby catching the tooth of the paper and allowing the colour beneath to show through. Layers of colour can be built up in this way, each layer modifying the tone and colour of the previous one. On highly textured papers similar effects can be obtained by rolling the brush over the surface. Scumbled paint is applied in a rough, circular, scrubbing motion; this is tough on expensive watercolour brushes, so you may want to use an old or cheaper brush for the job. This technique is used primarily for describing textures, but is also a handy way to put interest into an area of flat colour.

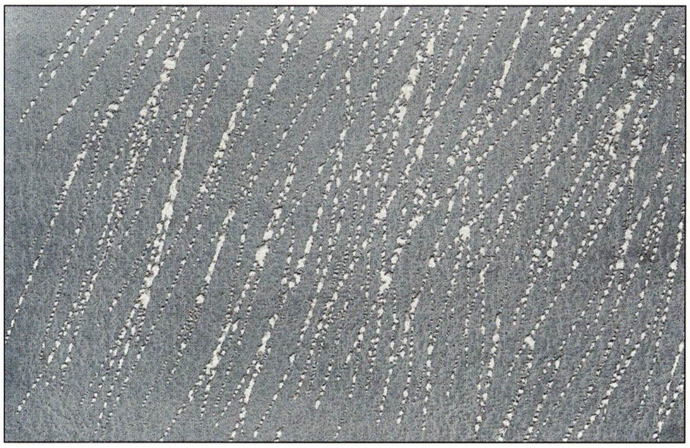

▲ Sgraffito is a method whereby the artist scratches or scrapes into a layer of paint, exposing what is beneath. This could be paper or another layer of paint. The word sgraffito comes from the Italian word *graffiare*, which means to scratch. This technique can be employed to scratch in highlights (by exposing the white paper) or used to create texture. Any sharp instrument can be used, as can your fingernail or a piece of sandpaper. Working into these marks with more paint will create even further effects, as paint dries to a different colour on paper surfaces that have been distressed.

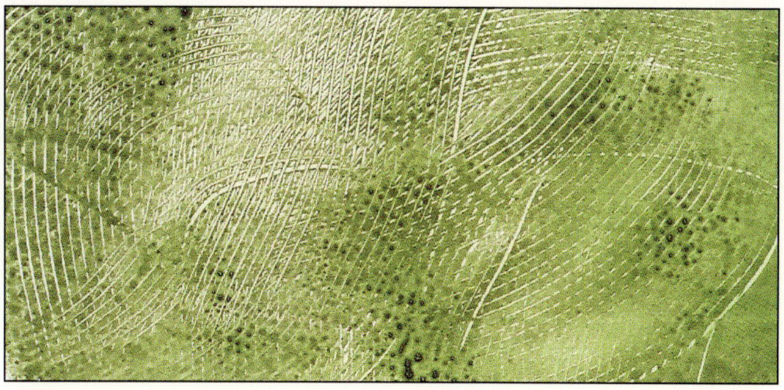

▲ The more a paper is sized, the less the paint will soak into and stain the surface. Papers such as blotting paper are not sized at all. On papers that are heavily sized or given a coat of gesso and on watercolour and illustration boards, it is possible to use paint that is thickened with gum arabic or aquapasto. The paint, when applied, is thick enough to retain the shape of the brush mark and can be worked and scratched into with painting knives, bits of wood, combs and coarse brushes – in fact anything that will make an impression.

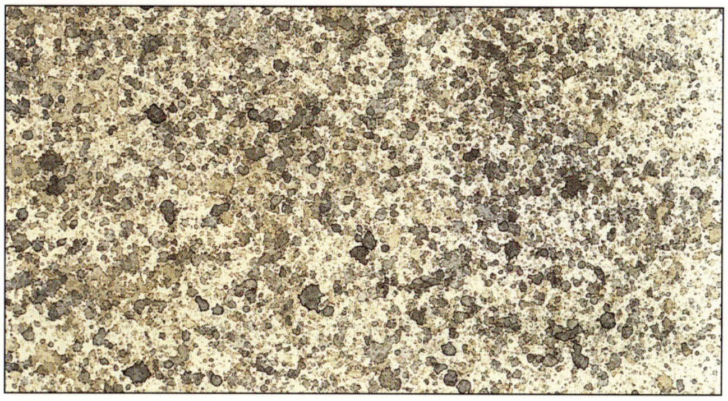

▲ There are three methods of spattering a painting, each having a very different and distinct feel and use. The first is to spatter paint onto a dry surface, where the spattering is then allowed to dry. The spattered marks will have a crisp outline and can be overworked with more spattering if required. In this way a dense, complex area of small blobs of paint can be built-up. The second method is to spatter into a wet or damp surface. As the spattered paint or clean water hits the wet paper it diffuses and softens in much the same way as paint used wet into wet does. The degree of bleed depends on the dampness of the surface. The third method is to spatter clean water onto a dry painted surface that has had plenty of gum arabic added to the mix. Gum arabic has the effect of keeping the dry paint soluble, so that it loosens and dissolves when rewet. These spatters can be left to become dry and lighter in tone, contained by a distinct watermark. Alternatively, once the paint is dissolved, you can blot them with a kitchen towel, which will leave much paler, tidier marks. Use a tooth brush or stiff bristle brush to carry the paint for splattering. Once the brush is loaded, pull a finger (a knife blade can be used with the toothbrush) through the bristles, which will then spring back, flicking the paint off onto the surface. As a general rule, the spattering from the toothbrush will be finer and more easily controlled than that thrown from a larger bristle brush.

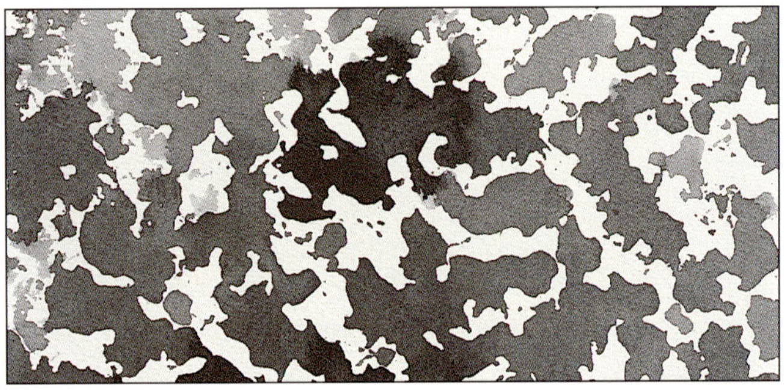

Sponges can be used to apply washes and broad areas of colour. They also can make a broad range of textures and effects. Both natural and synthetic sponges can be used; the natural ones are softer and the shape can be altered easily, making it possible to work in smaller areas. Mottled patterns can be built-up in layers or the sponge can be twisted and moved over the surface creating a series of marks that seem to pull in and out of focus. When dabbing the sponge to create a mottled effect, turn it constantly to present a different profile to the paper after each dab. This prevents the same shaped marks being made too close together. Wash your sponges well after use, so that colour does not harden in them, leading to unwanted smears of colour the next time they are used.

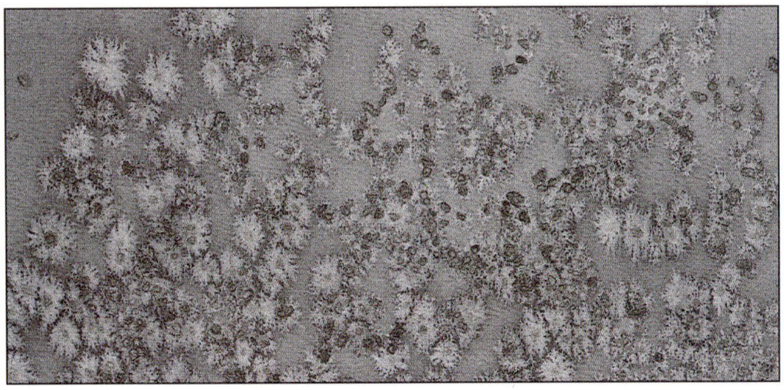

An interesting effect can be achieved by using rock salt. The salt crystals are sprinkled onto wet paint, where they soak up the surrounding paint. Once the painting is dry, the coarse salt is brushed from the surface, leaving a mottled effect that looks like the ice crystals that form on windows. The degree of success and definition depends on judging when to sprinkle the salt. Salt sprinkled onto paper that is too wet soaks up paint from some distance away, so the resulting mark tends to be larger, but indistinct. If you sprinkle the salt when the paper is too dry, very little happens.

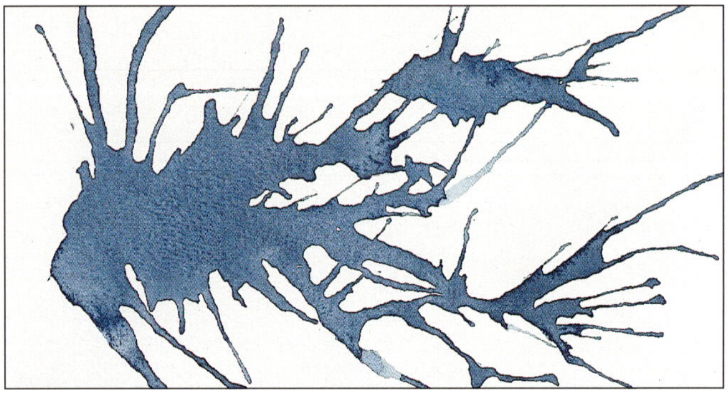

Blowing into wet paint will move it across the paper surface. This technique is a useful way to suggest the growth of some plants or the framework of branches in a tree. It is difficult to control the direction in which the paint will travel, but by blowing through a straw you will have more control over the spread of the paint, and can usually manipulate it in the general direction you would prefer it to go.

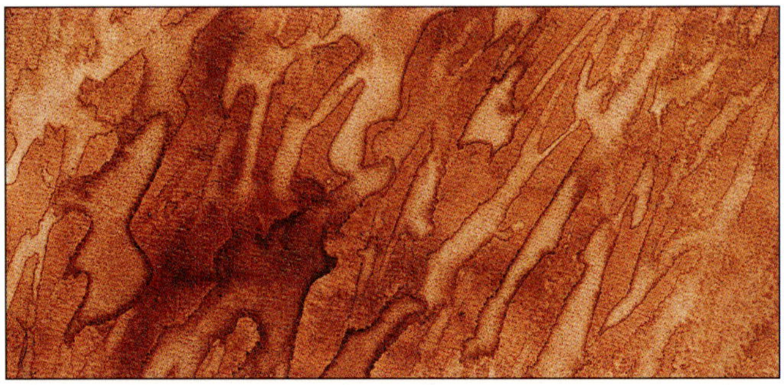

Gum arabic and gum water are the binders used in the manufacture of watercolour. Either one can be added to paint to enrich and intensify the colour. Once added the paint dries to a semi-gloss finish and holds brush marks better, so it should not be used when painting a large flat wash. The paint also remains very soluble when dry, so it can be rewet and removed or moved around. This means you can draw into areas using water, and the paint taken off by blotting or lifting out with a brush. It also means, however, that any area (even those that are meant to be kept) when washed over with water or more paint will soften and blend with the new layer; therefore a little forethought is needed, using the additive only in final stages, unless specific effects are required early on.

Pulling out highlights from areas of paint that has been mixed with gum water or gum arabic is easy. Simply rewet the area and once the paint loosens it can be blotted off with kitchen or blotting paper. If the highlight is small then use a brush. Very fine light lines can be introduced in this way, which makes it a perfect technique for portraits – individual strands of hair can be picked out, as can the sparkle in the eyes.

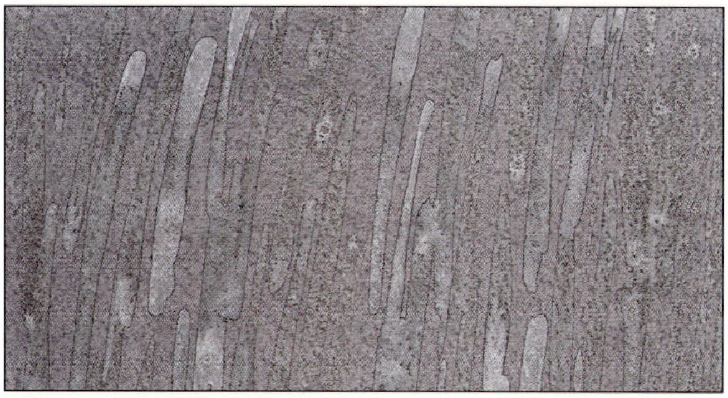

Domestic bleach will also lift paint that is difficult to dissolve. When brushed on it will gradually lighten the colour. It also tends to change the colour, giving it a slight blue tinge, so it would pay to experiment first on a spare piece of paper. The bleach is hard on brushes, so do not use your most expensive sable.

Sponges are also used to lift out colour, and are an invaluable tool for painting skies. A wet sponge can be used to dab into washes, in order to shape clouds and change colours. You will find that when working into damp or wet paint, colour will be picked up and removed more easily if the sponge is damp. The sponge can also be used for flooding areas with water to create backwashes.

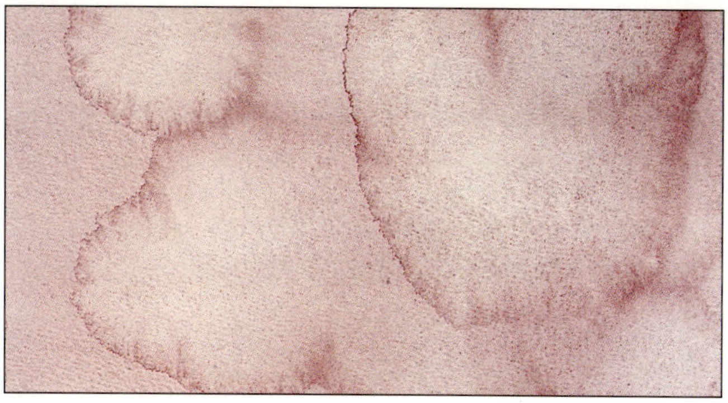

Backwashes happen when very wet paint or water is introduced onto an area that is not so wet. The difference in wetness means the areas dry at different speeds, resulting in a watermark where the fresh wet paint met and pushed back the older damp paint. These backwashes often happen when instead of leaving a wash alone and allowing it to dry, the artist tries to touch up an area. The backwash, or backrun, far from being a nuisance is actually a valuable and handy technique, helping put life and spontaneity into painted skies and landscape.

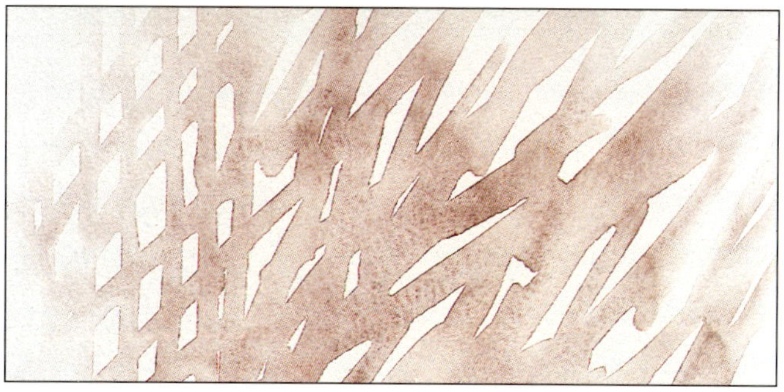

Here the shapes and lines have been painted in clean water, then, while still wet, a brush loaded with paint has been touched to the centre of the design. The paint flows from the brush into the wet areas, mixing with the water and gradually becoming more dilute and lighter in tone as it gets further away from the point where it was introduced. This technique can be used when painting complicated edges, allowing the paint to flow into the desired shape, but without bringing the brush too close to areas where paint is not wanted.

STRETCHING PAPER

THE LIGHTER WEIGHT, or thinner papers, and, to a lesser degree, some of the medium-weight papers, have a tendency to buckle, or cockle, when wet paint is applied. This means the paint puddles in the dips, drying unevenly and leaving unsightly watermarks – always where you least want them. The cockled paper also makes the application of flat washes impossible. To prevent this from occuring the watercolour paper is stretched onto a wooden board. There are several ways of doing this, but the simplest, and perhaps most efficient, is to use strips of gummed paper to secure the edges of the paper to the board. The gummed strips prevent the wet paper from moving so that it dries flat after each wash or layer of paint. Once the painting is finished and dry, the edge of the gummed strip is cut with a sharp knife, releasing the paper.

Stretching paper is very easy, but some papers stretch more easily than others. Thin papers can be awkward, so practise with easier, medium-weight papers such as Bockingford or Saunders.

The Techniques

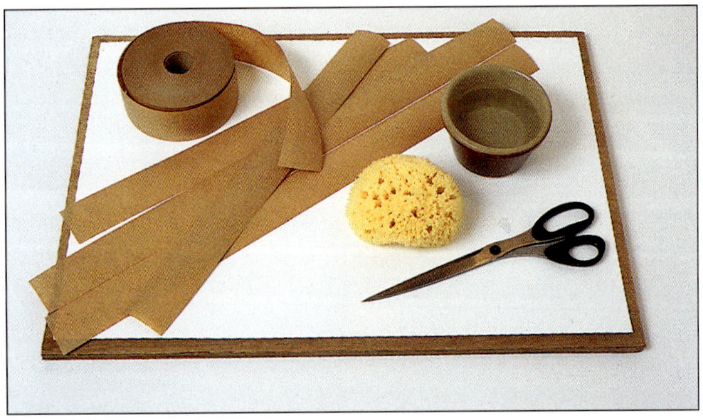

▲ You will need a smooth board that is thick enough to resist warping, such as a drawing board or a piece of waterproof, medium-density fibre board, a roll of gummed paper, a clean sponge, water, a pair of scissors and a sheet of watercolour paper. Tear or cut the sheet of paper to the required size and cut four lengths of gummed paper, one for each edge of the paper.

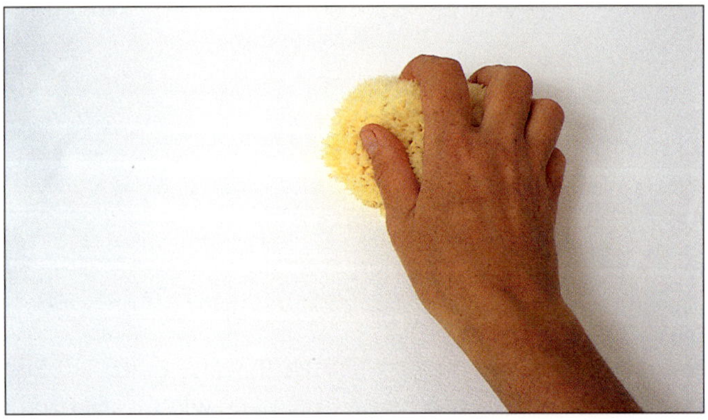

▲ Check that the correct side of the paper is uppermost; if the paper has a watermark this should read the right way round when the paper is held up to the light. Alternatively, look for a slight sheen on the paper's surface, as this indicates the side that is sized and ready to receive paint. Position the sheet of paper centrally on the board and load the sponge well with water. Squeeze the water onto the paper and, using the sponge gently so as not to damage the paper's surface, spread the water evenly over it until it is reasonably damp, but not soaking wet.

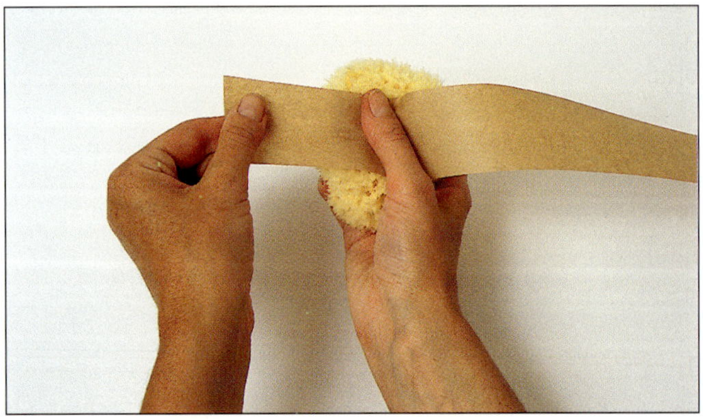

▲ Wet a length of gummed paper by simply pulling it across the damp sponge.

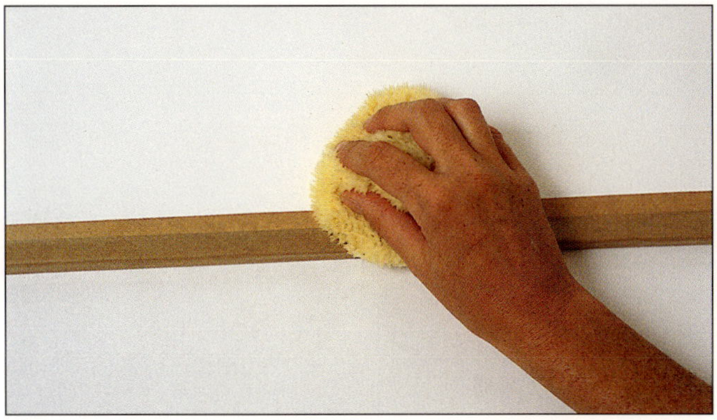

▲
Then, using the sponge, smooth the paper strip along one edge of the paper so that about a half to one-third of its width sticks to the paper and the rest sticks to the board. Smoothing the gummed strip around and down the side edges of the board means that the paper cannot be pulled off no matter how taut it becomes.

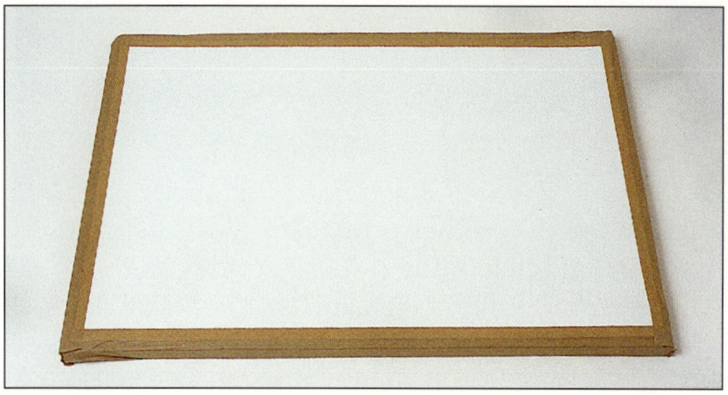

▲
The paper will begin to cockle, so work quickly and secure the other sides. Wipe off any excess moisture with the sponge and let the board dry. If the paper surface looks uneven and crinkled don't worry – once dry it will be flat and taut. Speed up drying by using a hair dryer, but keep it moving over the paper surface so that the sheet dries at an even rate all over.

COLOUR

THE PRIMARY COLOURS red, yellow and blue cannot be mixed from other colours, hence their name. Red and yellow make orange; yellow and blue, green; and blue and red make purple or violet – these are known as secondaries. But, as a casual glance at a paint colour chart will show, there are many different reds, yellows and blues, and the secondary colours obtained will depend very much on which of these primaries are used. The same applies to tertiary colours, which are the colours that fall between the primaries and the secondaries. They are made by mixing an equal amount of a primary colour with an equal amount of the secondary next to it to obtain a red-orange, orange-yellow, yellow-green, green-blue, blue-violet or violet-red.

All colours are considered to be either warm or cool – the warm colours are red, orange and yellow; the cool colours are green, blue and violet. However, the terms warm and cool are relative, as all colours have a warm and cool variant. There are warm reds such as cadmium, which have a yellow bias, and cool reds such as alizarin crimson, which have a blue bias. To confuse the issue further, a colour that is seen as warm in isolation can appear cool when seen next to a warmer variant of a similar colour. This warm-cool colour relationship is very important and can be put to good use, especially when painting the landscape, as warm colours seem to advance visually and cool colours appear to recede.

When mixing colours it is necessary to remember that a more intense, brighter third colour will result if mixed from two colours that have a bias toward each other: for example cadmium red (yellow bias) and cadmium yellow (red bias) create a bright, vivid orange, whereas alizarin crimson (blue bias) and cadmium yellow (red bias) mix to create a more subdued, less intense orange. This happens because alizarin crimson is closer to yellow's complementary colour, violet.

Complementary colours are those colours that fall opposite one another on the colour wheel; one colour will always have a warm bias, the other will have a cool bias. Hence, red is the complementary of green and orange is the complementary of blue. These colour opposites are known as complementary pairs and have a very special relationship. When placed next to each other, complementary pairs have the effect of enhancing or intensifying each other. However, if you mix a small amount of a colour into its complementary, the colour will be subdued or knocked back. Add more of a colour's complementary colour and you will neutralise it completely, producing a range of neutral greys and browns. It is important to be able to mix and exploit these less vivid, subdued colours, as they echo many of the colours seen in nature and help bring colour harmony to the work.

Tone is measured on a scale that runs from black to white, and all colours can be mixed to obtain a range of tones. Obtaining a lighter tone in watercolour is especially easy, as once a colour is mixed all you need to do is add more water until the desired lighter value is achieved. Remember, however, that if you choose to darken the tone of a colour by adding black, or another dark colour, as well as becoming darker the colour will also change.

Colour is a complex and intriguing subject and a basic knowledge of the theory is certainly necessary, but the best way to understand what is possible, and why, is to spend time experimenting with your colours. Do remember to make notes, as the combinations using just a few colours are countless and the chances of mixing a colour and immediately forgetting how you did it is a real possibility.

Choosing Colours

Watercolours are available in over 80 different colours, but it is neither economically viable, practical or necessary to work with anywhere near that many. Most professional artists work with a limited palette; my own is fairly large and consists of 18 colours, but rarely do I use more than 12 at any one time, and often get by with half that number. The colours that are marked with an asterisk are an ideal choice for a starter palette, which you can add to should you feel the need at a later date.

IVORY BLACK should be used with caution as it can very easily deaden a colour, but it is useful when mixed with yellows to create a range of greens

PAYNE'S GRAY* is used to knock back and modify colours without destroying their vitality

COBALT BLUE* is a good blue for skies and it is also a useful addition to cool down skin tones

ULTRAMARINE* is a strong, powerful warm blue, which mixes well with reds to create purples and violets

ANTWERP BLUE is a pale version of Prussian blue, which is very transparent. It is good for skies and mixing bright greens

CERULEAN BLUE is an opaque colour good for mixing into skies and granulated washes

VIRIDIAN* is possibly the only green that is really needed. It is a very powerful, transparent green, which mixes well with reds, yellows and browns to create a vast range of greens

SAP GREEN is a bright, easily modified green for landscape work

OXIDE OF CHROMIUM is a very opaque, permanent colour, which is good for modifying other colours, especially skin tones. Mixed with reds it creates a range of browns

NAPLES YELLOW is a semi-opaque colour, which is very useful when painting the figure and portraits

LEMON YELLOW* is a cool yellow, which creates bright greens when mixed with blues

CADMIUM YELLOW* is a strong, warm yellow, which mixes well with blue to create warm greens, and with reds creating a range of orange

YELLOW OCHRE* is a strong and useful opaque yellow. Some artists prefer to use the similar, but darker and more transparent, raw sienna

BURNT UMBER is a very warm brown, which mixes well with other colours, especially green. It makes a good black when mixed with Payne's gray

RAW UMBER is a versatile colour, which can be used to tone down other more strident colours

ALIZARIN CRIMSON* mixes well with Naples yellow and yellow ochre, giving a range of skin tones. It also combines well with the various blues to provide purple and violet

CADMIUM RED* is a strong red. It makes a good orange and mixes well with green to create a range of browns

BROWN MADDER ALIZARIN is an extremely useful dull red, which mixes well with the duller yellows, giving good skin tones

Colour Theory – The Basics

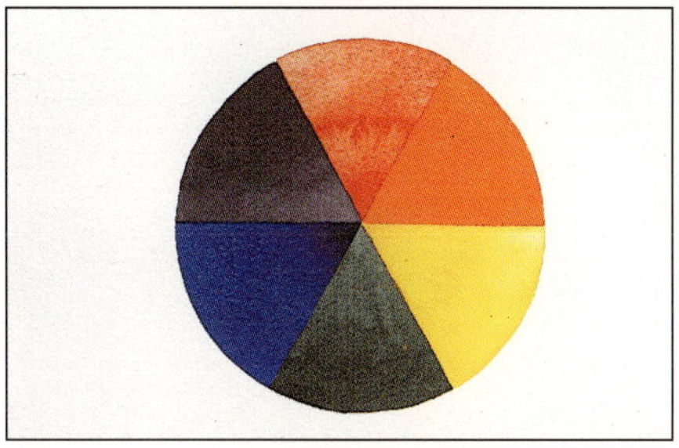

This colour wheel is mixed using warm primaries: cadmium red, cadmium yellow and ultramarine.

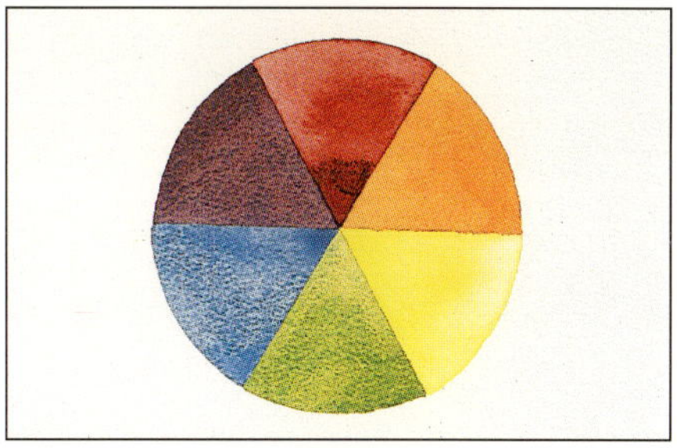

Here the secondaries have been mixed using the cool primaries: alizarin crimson, lemon yellow and cerulean blue.

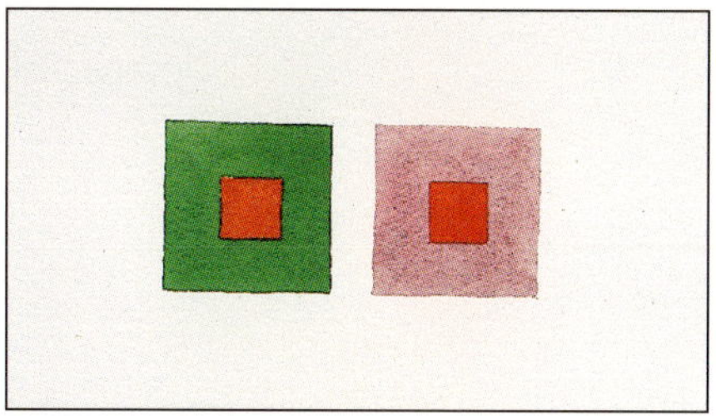

A colour is noticeably affected by the colour that is next to it. Here the red square seems to be much brighter when surrounded by its complementary green.

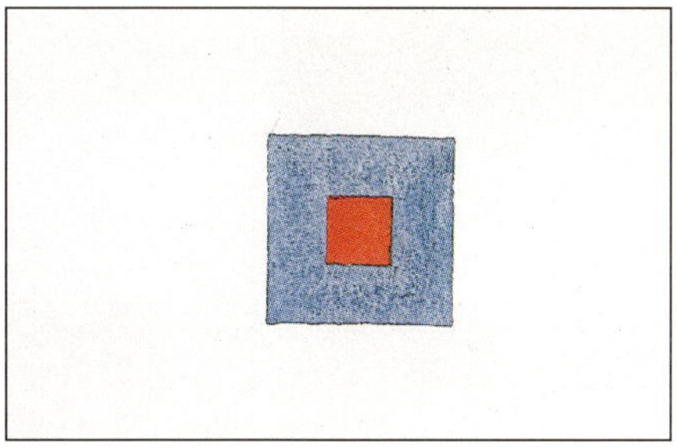

Warm colours will seem to advance and cool colours recede.

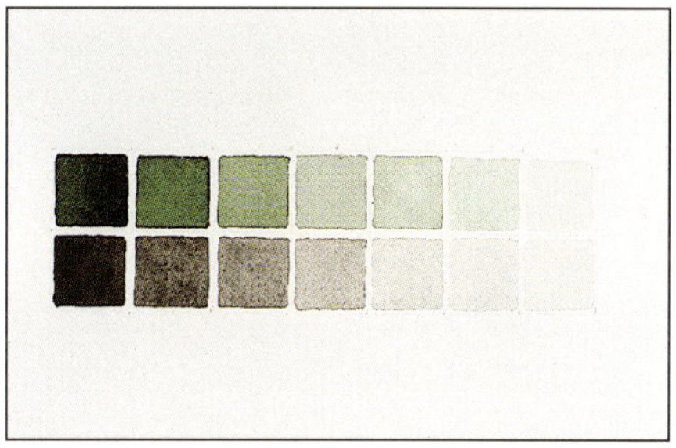

All tonal values have an equivalent on a scale that runs from black through to white. The tone of this green has been lightened by adding clean water.

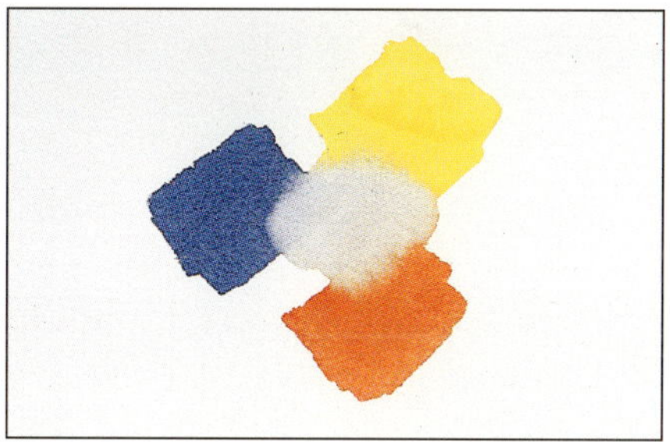

Mixing together complementary colours (as shown here), which will contain elements of all three primaries, will result in a range of neutral greys.

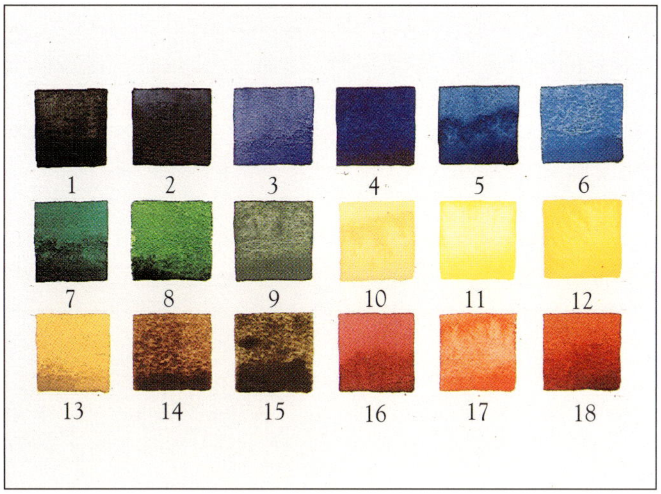

My palette of colours.

1 Ivory Black
2 Payne's Gray
3 Cobalt Blue
4 Ultramarine
5 Antwerp Blue
6 Cerulean Blue
7 Viridian
8 Sap Green
9 Oxide of Chromium
10 Naples Yellow
11 Lemon Yellow
12 Cadmium Yellow
13 Yellow Ochre
14 Burnt Umber
15 Raw Umber
16 Alizarin Crimson
17 Cadmium Red
18 Brown Madder Alizarin

THE SOUTH DOWNS

Using Washes

PROJECT ONE

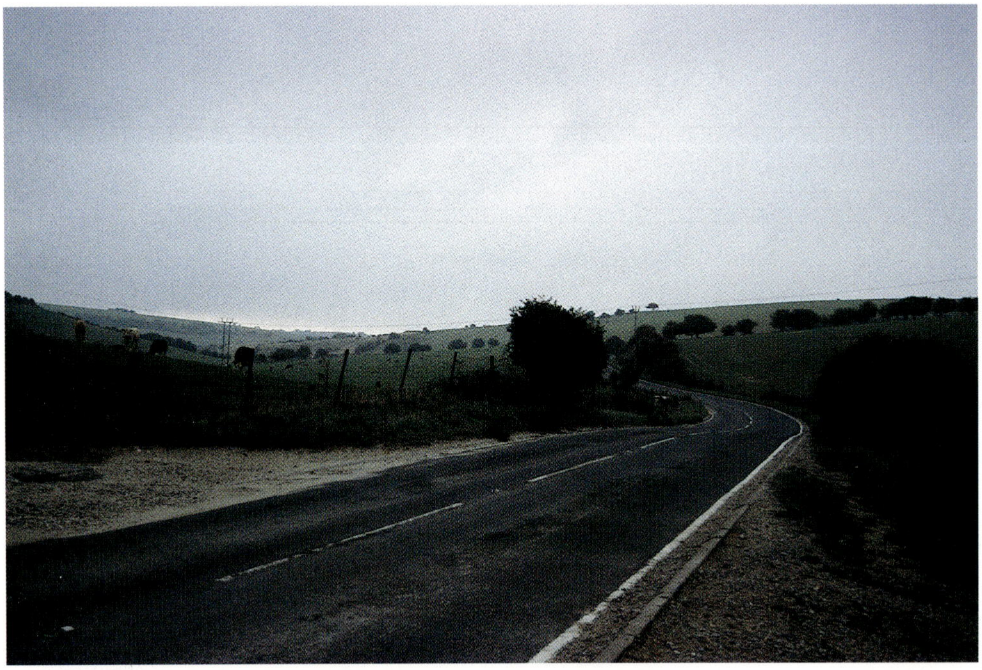

WATERCOLOUR IS A TRANSPARENT MEDIUM; the colours and tones are laid, or glazed, in thin washes over one another. To prevent the colours becoming a muddy and meaningless mess, each layer is usually allowed to dry before the next is added. Another wash of the same colour can then be applied, which has the effect of strengthening the colour or tone, or a wash of a different colour can be used – this will modify and alter the colour or tone. For this reason watercolours are painted light to dark. The lightest, palest tones and colours are applied first, followed layer by layer with stronger, darker, often less transparent colours.

Overpaint too much and a watercolour will loose its freshness, so try to achieve the desired effect with a maximum of three or four washes (or layers) of paint. A colour is lightened not by adding white paint but by adding water, which makes the colour more transparent and thinner, allowing more light to reflect back through the paint from the surface of the white paper. The paper itself supplies the white and any highlights needed, so a little thought and pre-planning are required to make sure that these areas are not accidentally covered with paint.

Landscape, as countless artists have discovered, is rich, diverse and stimulating and, as a subject, is perfectly suited to the wash techniques of traditional watercolour. This view, looking across the English South Downs on an overcast, misty autumn morning, is a relatively straightforward and simple subject with which to work. The dark bush just off-centre gives an immediate focal point and the road and fence posts running into the picture and the receding dark clouds give both linear and aerial perspectives. The range of colour is limited and the scene is not overfussed with too much detail.

MATERIALS AND EQUIPMENT

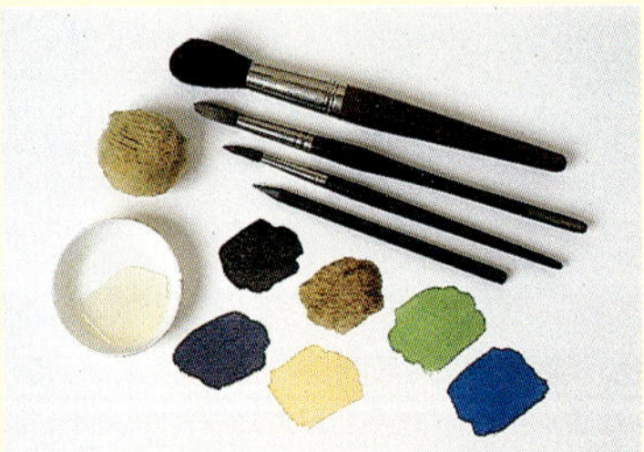

15x22in sheet of stretched 200lb (425gsm) CP Bockingford watercolour paper
Medium-size mop or wash brush

Two round brushes, no 12 and no 6
HB graphite stick
Small natural sponge
Gum arabic

Watercolours in the following colours: ivory black, Payne's gray, raw umber, yellow ochre, sap green and Antwerp blue

The Painting

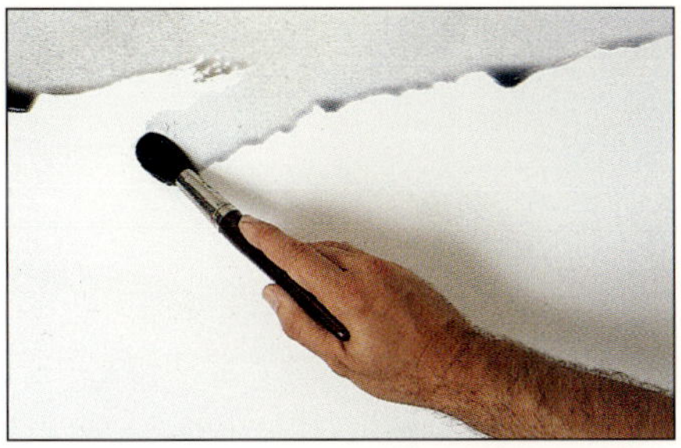

1 You may find that a light drawing made with an HB pencil gives you confidence in correctly positioning the horizon line and the curve of the road. With the support at a slight angle, begin by painting in the grey overcast sky with a thin mixture of Payne's gray, yellow ochre and raw umber, using the medium-size mop or wash brush. The paint is loosely washed onto the support and pulled across the sky area, leaving patches of the paper showing through to represent the white of clouds.

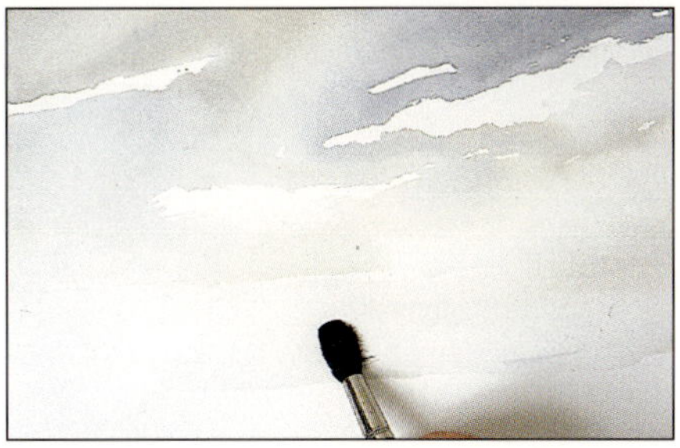

2 As the horizon line is approached the mix is lightened by adding more water and the colour altered by adding a little more yellow ochre; bring the wash well down below the line of the fields. Already you have introduced perspective into the painting: the darker colour at the top suggests that the sky at this point is nearer, more overhead, while the lighter colour gives the impression that the sky is receding away in the distance.

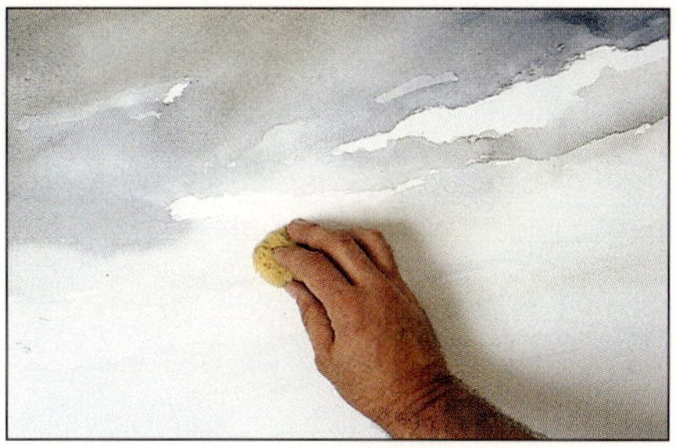

3 Once dry rework the sky to intensify the colour. Rewet the area with a sponge and clean water and, starting at the top right hand corner, introduce a wash of Payne's gray and Antwerp blue using the large brush; the paint will naturally run into the wet areas. Pull the wash across the sky, leaving some areas of cloud as white paper, but working lightly over others. The sponge is used to knock back, or lighten, areas that are considered to be too dark and to soften any paint edges around the horizon.

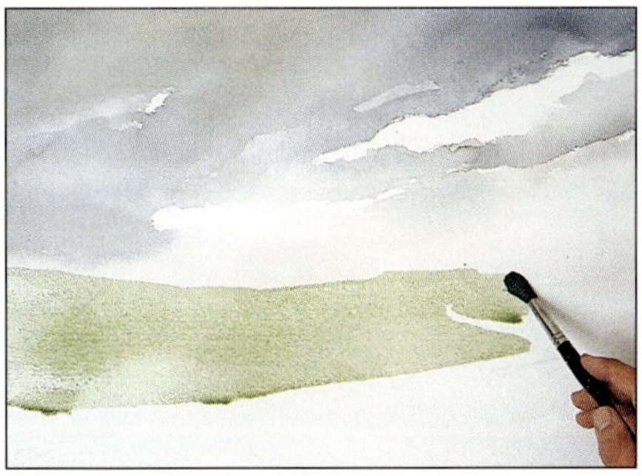

4 Once the sky has been allowed to dry thoroughly, a thin mix made from sap green and yellow ochre, with a little raw umber added to deaden the colour, is washed in across the area of fields, taking care not to paint over the position of the road. Use the no 12 round brush; because the sky is no longer wet, the green wash will dry giving a crisp edge at the horizon.

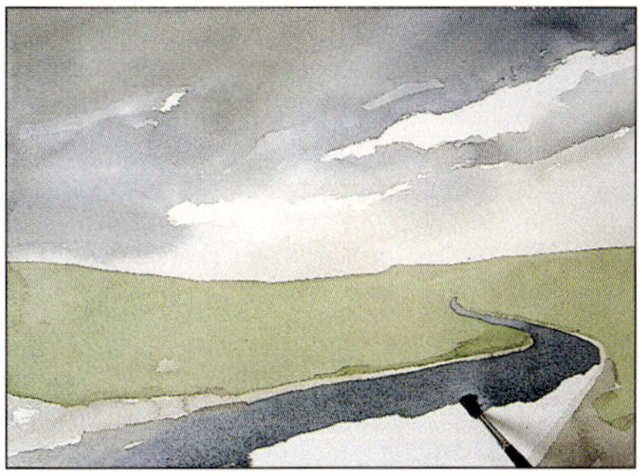

5 Once the fields are dry, use the no 6 round brush to paint the edge of the road with a mix of yellow ochre and a little ivory black. When dry, use the same brush for washing in the road with Payne's gray dulled with a little ivory black.

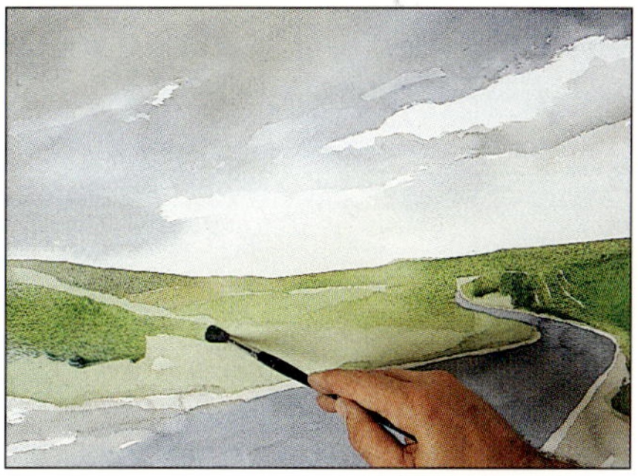

6 When the road has dried, mix sap green, yellow ochre and Payne's gray to make a light grey-green. Paint in the pattern of the fields, varying the mix by adding more sap green and yellow ochre. At the roadside work into the light green underpainting to suggest tufts of long grass.

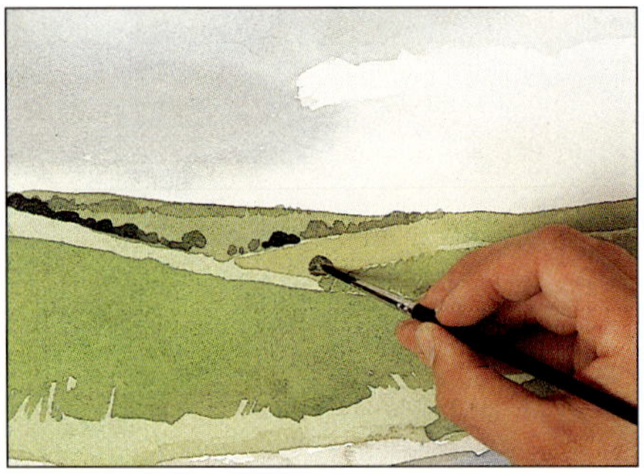

7 Once the fields are dry, use a slightly darker shade of green and work back into them, painting in the lines of crops with the no 6 round brush. Curving the lines slightly gives the impression that the crops are growing up and over the hill. Mix up a few shades of green with the yellow ochre, sap green, Payne's gray and raw umber and work across the landscape, dotting in trees and hedgerows, varying the colours as you work. Mixing in a little gum arabic will sharpen and intensify the colour.

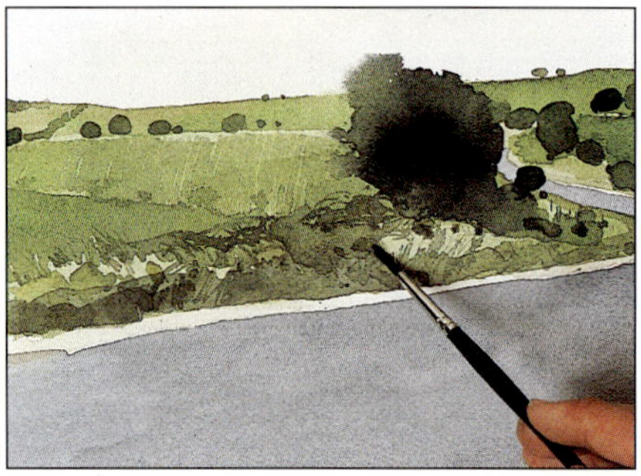

8 The focal point of the picture – the large dark bush – is painted next. The shape is made by dabbing the natural sponge, wet but not sodden, over the area and touching in a dark mix of Payne's gray and sap green with the no 12 round brush. The paint flows from the brush, easily finding its own way into the shape left by the wet sponge. Changing back to the no 6 round brush, paint in the curve of the brambles and flick in tufts of long grass along the road side with dark green.

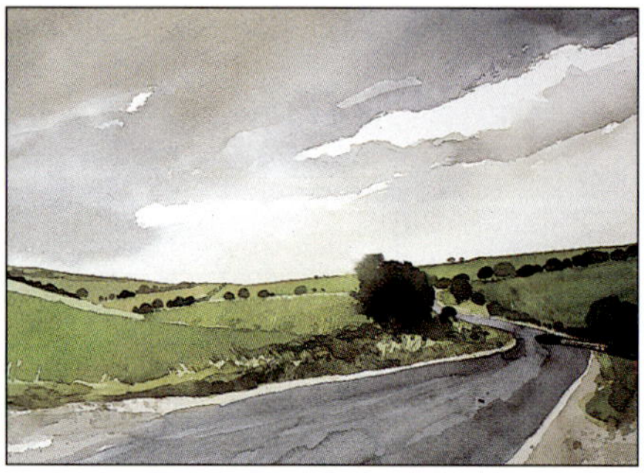

9 Using the no 6 round brush, the road surface is given interest by washing over it in part with Payne's gray and ivory black. The watermarks are created in the foreground by allowing the paint to dry a little and then brushing on a touch of clean water.

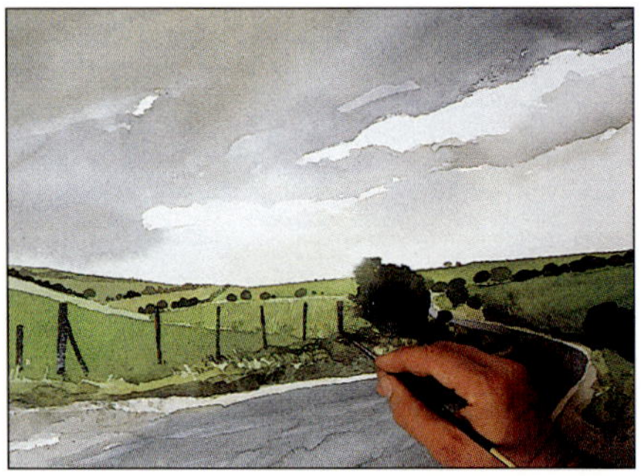

10 Still using the no 6 round brush, paint in the fence posts with a dark mix made from raw umber and ivory black. Paint the bottom of each post as if it disappears behind and into the long grass.

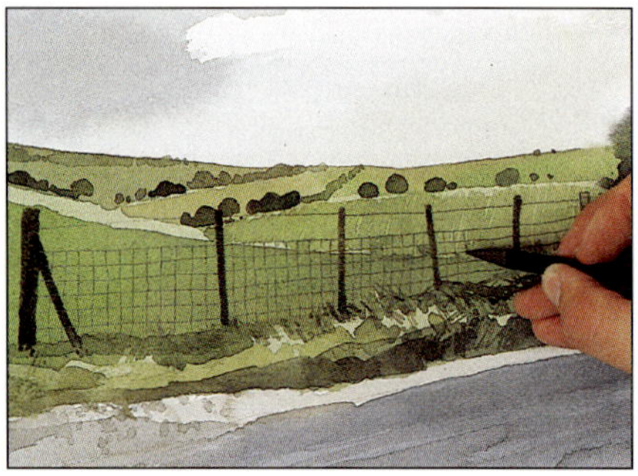

11 The mesh of the wire netting stretched taut between the posts is drawn in with the HB graphite stick.

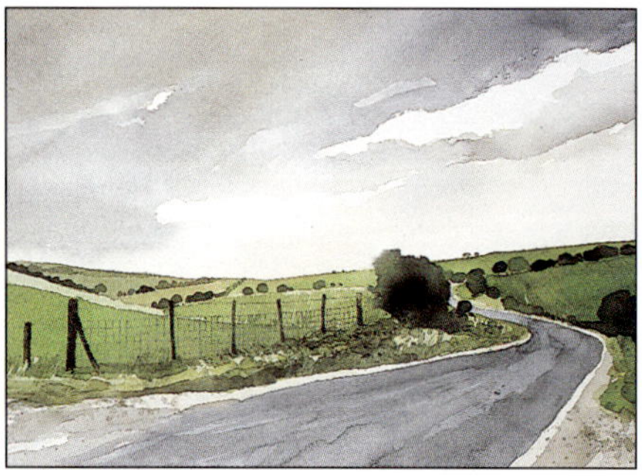

12 The painting is completed by adding extra interest with more grass at the road side and along the foot of the fence and by painting in the suggestion of crop rows curving over the field on the extreme right.

Alternative Approaches

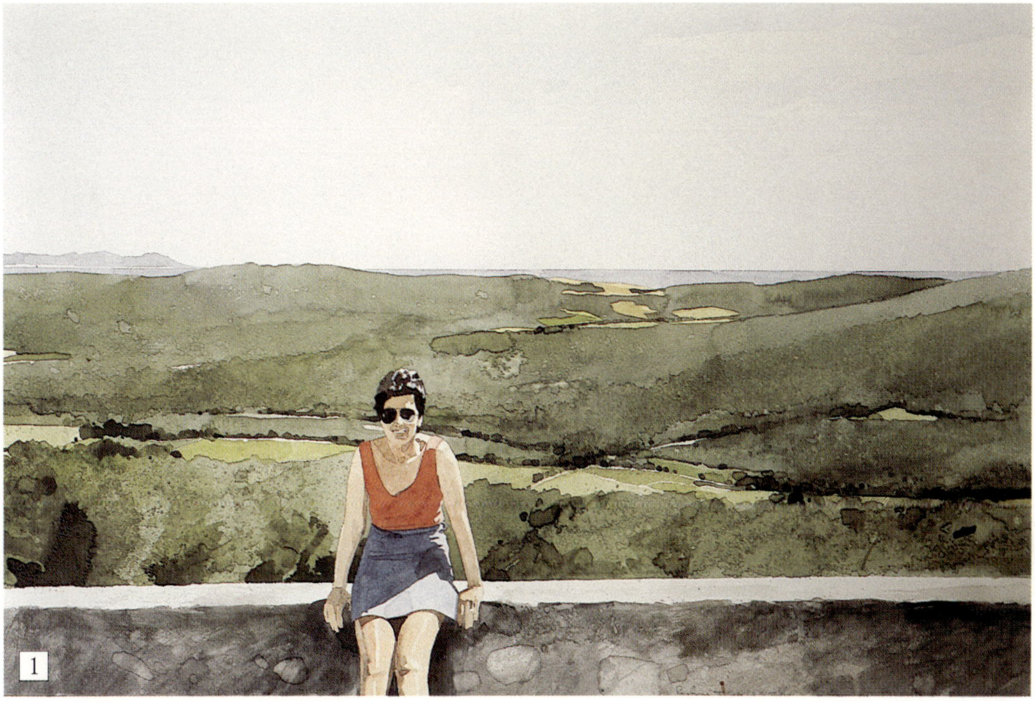

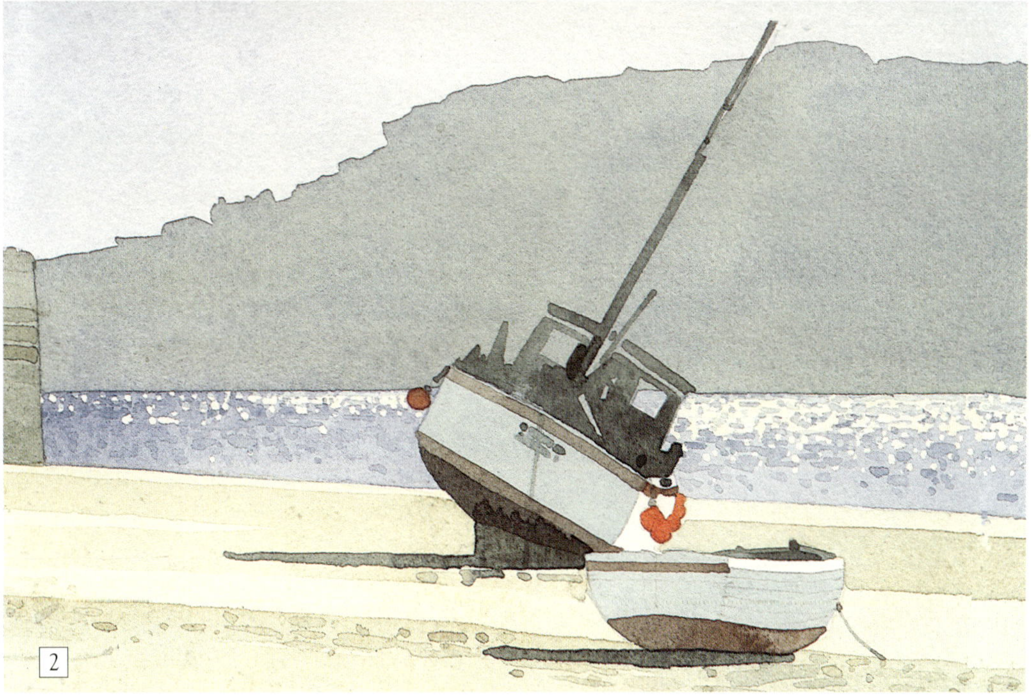

1 The distance is painted in cool, pale blue washes creating the illusion of aerial perspective. The landscape rolling away to the distant sea is covered in a variety of subtle textures, which suggest wooded areas and fields, while the brighter warm colours on the figure bring it firmly to the fore.

2 In this painting of boats on the low-tide beach in St Ives, Cornwall, each wash is worked wet on dry; the tones are carefully considered, helping give an illusion of depth. The sparkle on the water is achieved by using masking fluid to protect the white paper.

VEGETABLES

Combining Techniques

PROJECT TWO

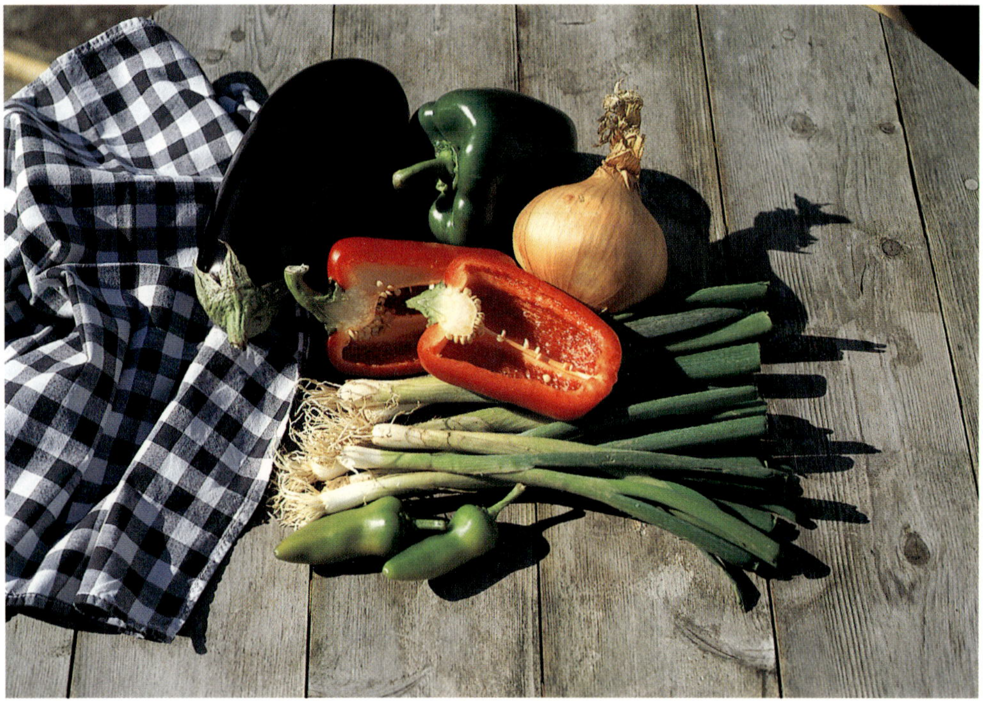

SELDOM, IF EVER, IS A PAINTING COMPLETED using one technique only; more often than not the finished picture is the result of several techniques, each playing its own important part. While it is possible to produce a painting using only wet into wet, that is, working onto damp or wet paper or paint – the painting will look soft and out of focus, with no firm structure or form. The purity of the colours will be difficult to control, because they will run and blend together, and, in places where too many different colours had mixed, they would become muddy and unrecognisable. It also becomes difficult to work light to dark because a wet, dark colour placed next to or over a wet, light colour will run and bleed uncontrollably into it, spoiling the effect.

Painting a picture using only wet on dry techniques, where each layer or area of paint is allowed to dry before another is placed over or adjacent to it, can also have its problems. Each layer or area of paint dries to shape, leaving an edge; working colour and tone light to dark in layers does not present any problems, but the colours stay where they are put, so random or controlled running and blending together of colour and the use of lost edges becomes difficult.

This painting of vegetables uses a combination of both techniques: the initial laying in of the overall shape, allowing colour to blend together, is done wet into wet. The image is then sharpened and pulled into focus by subsequent layers of paint worked wet over dry. This is a classic technique much favoured by landscape artists who find the initial wet into wet laying in of colour perfect for capturing the effects of atmosphere and weather.

MATERIALS AND EQUIPMENT

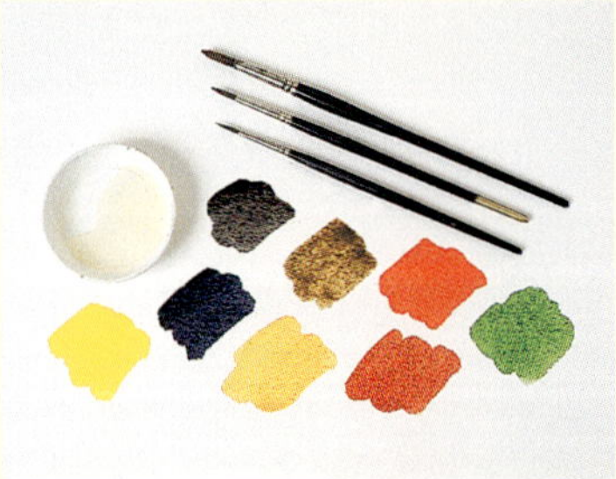

- 15x22in sheet of stretched 200lb (425gsm) CP Bockingford watercolour paper
- Three round brushes, no 8, no 5 and no 2
- Gum arabic
- Watercolours in the following colours: ivory black, Payne's gray, cadmium yellow, raw umber, yellow ochre, cadmium red, brown madder alizarin and sap green

The Painting

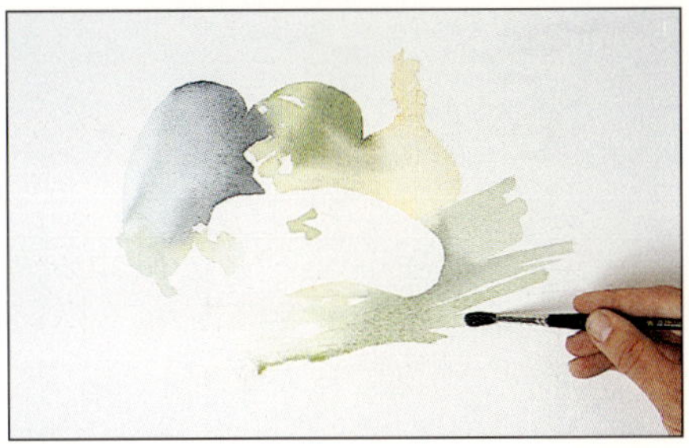

1 A light drawing executed with an HB pencil positions the vegetables and napkin on the table. The main shapes are then blocked in using the no 8 brush and pale mixes using Payne's gray, sap green and yellow ochre. Note how the lightest tone seen on each vegetable is painted first, and the position of any white highlights are left as white paper. The colour of an object is affected and altered by the reflected colour from other objects that are placed close by; working the initial light washes wet into wet and allowing the colours to bleed together hints at this and helps to create an overall harmony.

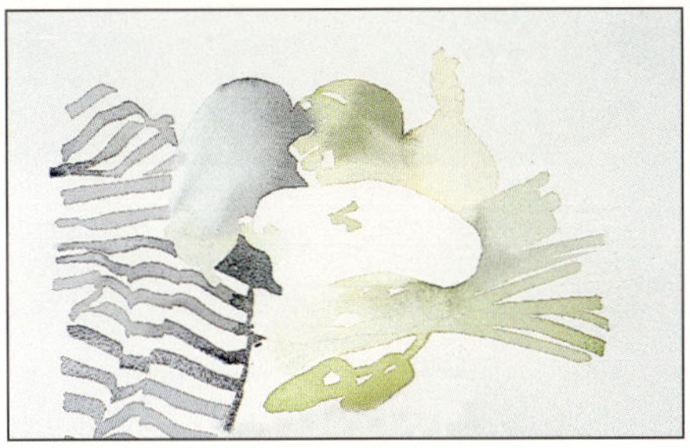

2 A pale mix of Payne's gray and ivory black is used for the pattern on the napkin. Using the no 5 brush, paint this by carefully following the contours of the cloth. Darken the mix slightly and paint in the shadow down the edge of the cloth. Allow the painting to dry.

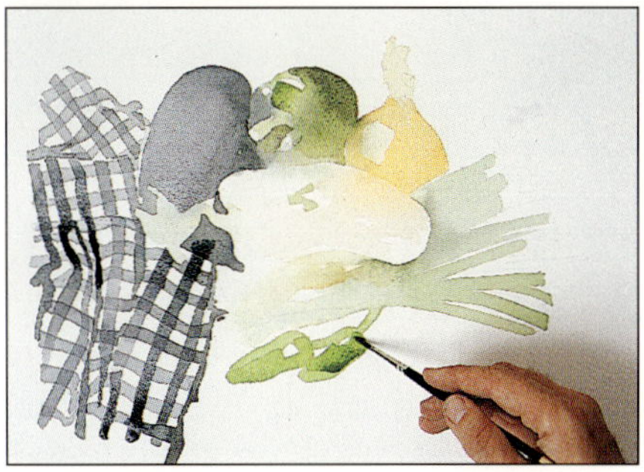

3 Darken the Payne's gray and ivory black mix a little and paint in the cross-over pattern again, taking care to follow the contours of the cloth. With the same mix work over the aubergine, leaving a light edge down the left-hand side and cutting around the green of the stem. Add a little cadmium red to yellow ochre and sharpen up the bulb of the onion, leaving the previous wash showing as a highlight. A very light wash of cadmium red is brushed over the peppers. Then sap green and a little Payne's gray intensifies the colour on the far pepper and darkens the underside of the small green chillies in the foreground.

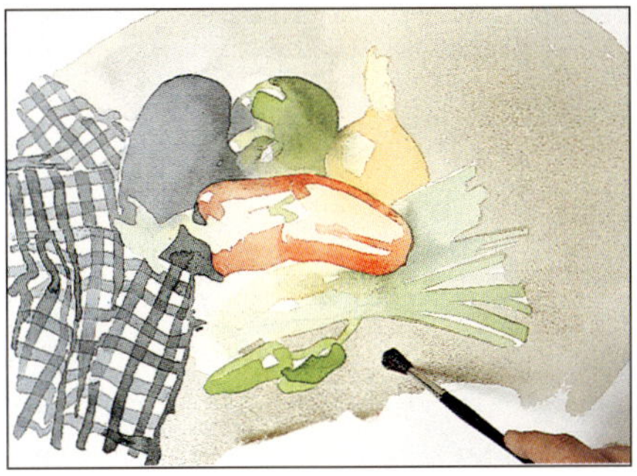

4 Using the no 8 brush and a mix of cadmium red, brown madder alizarin and a little cadmium yellow, block in the flesh and skin of the red peppers, then establish the base colour of the table top with a raw umber and ivory black mix. Allow the painting to dry.

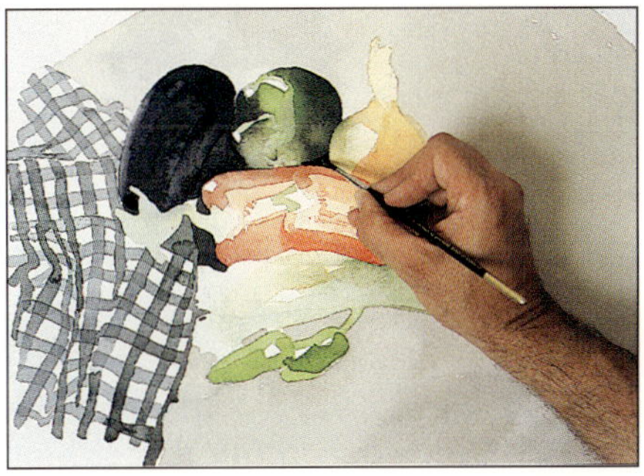

5 With the no 5 brush, the colour of the aubergine is darkened using Payne's gray mixed with a little brown madder alizarin. Add some of the gum arabic as well to increase the intensity of the colour. Let the aubergine dry and brush on water in the position of any highlights – the paint will dissolve and dry to a lighter colour. Add ivory black to the mix and paint in the shadows around the peppers. This has the effect of crisping up their shape and pushing them forward. Darken the shadow on the far pepper with a mix of sap green and Payne's gray, and put a darker wash of ochre and cadmium red over the shadowed side of the onion.

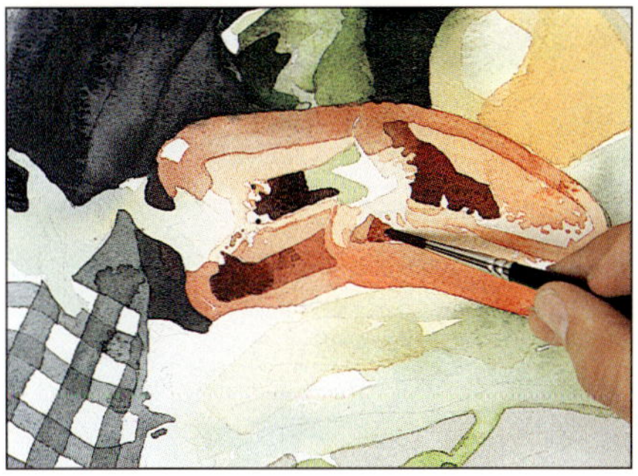

6 With the same brush, use a darkish mix of brown madder alizarin and a little Payne's gray to work the shadows inside the red peppers, working carefully and cutting in around the lighter seeds.

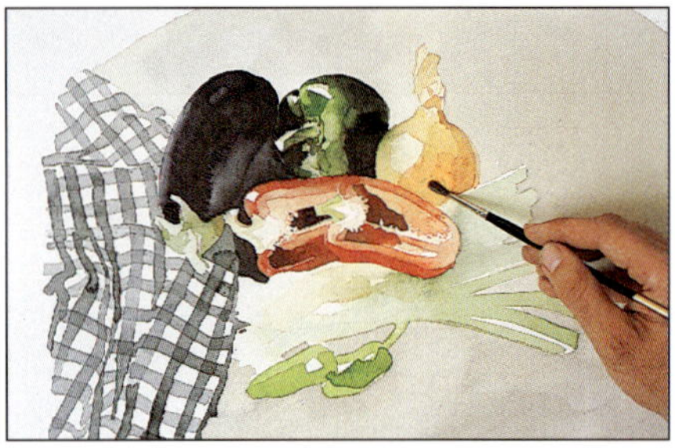

7 Working around the highlight, paint the bright green mid tones on the top of the pepper. Adding a little brown madder alizarin gives the warm green found on the underside of the pepper stalk, which is picking up some reflected colour from the red pepper. Use the same range of colour on the stalks of the aubergine and the red pepper. The crumpled skin of the onion is reworked with a mixture of ochre, cadmium red and raw umber.

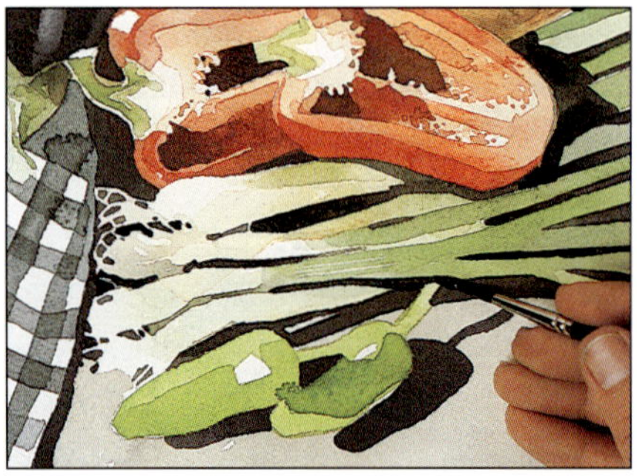

10 With the same dark mix begin to paint the dark spaces around and through the spring onion roots and the shadows that are cast across them from the red pepper. The same mix can then be used to darken the pattern on the napkin where the bands of grey cross each other.

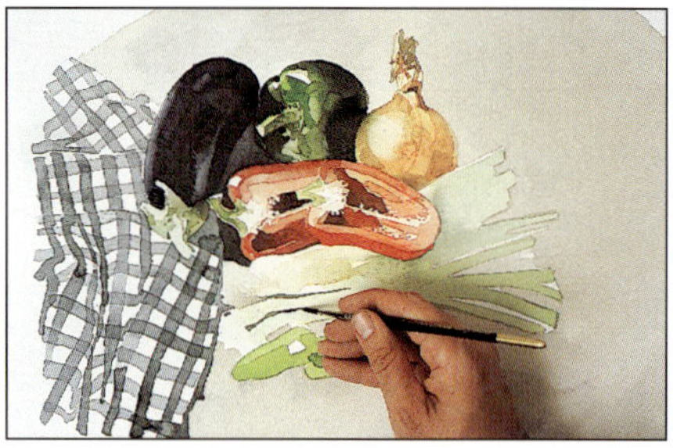

8 Then with a yellow ochre, raw umber and black mix begin to separate and define the shape of the individual spring onions.

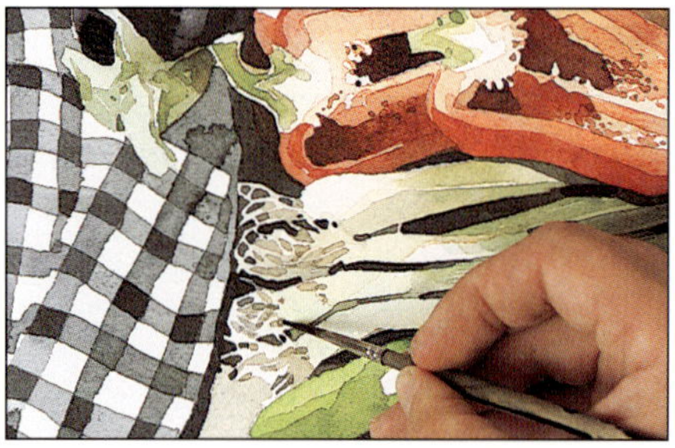

11 Brown madder alizarin adds more texture to the inside of the peppers' interiors. Mix raw umber, yellow ochre and ivory black and, using the no 2 brush, work on the roots of the onions. With a mix of yellow ochre and sap green paint in the ribs of colour that run down the onions' leaves.

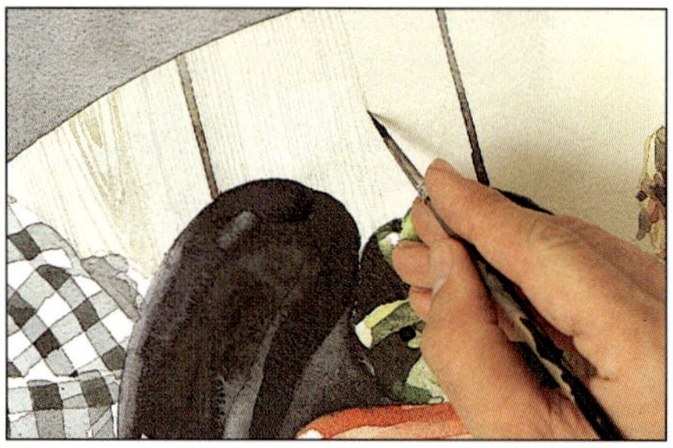

13 Finish by painting the grain on the table. Use a ruler if you wish in order to get the straight lines where the pieces of wood join, then use a combination of thin painted lines, using dilute raw umber and yellow ochre, and lines drawn with the HB graphite stick.

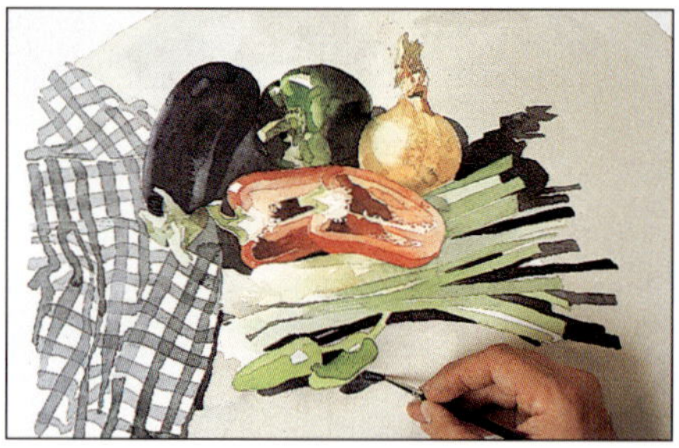

9 Still using the no 5 brush, mix sap green with yellow ochre and paint in the green on the spring onion stalks. Next, take Payne's gray, to which you have added a little ivory black, and work carefully around the vegetables, painting in the shadows.

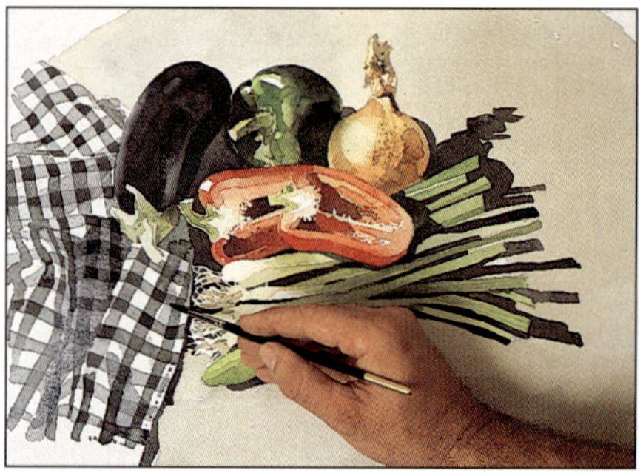

12 Using the no 5 brush, add some detail to the neck of the onion with a mix of raw umber and brown madder alizarin, then add interest to the skin on the bulb by spattering with a little of the same mix. The folds on the napkin are painted next with a medium-strength mix of grey.

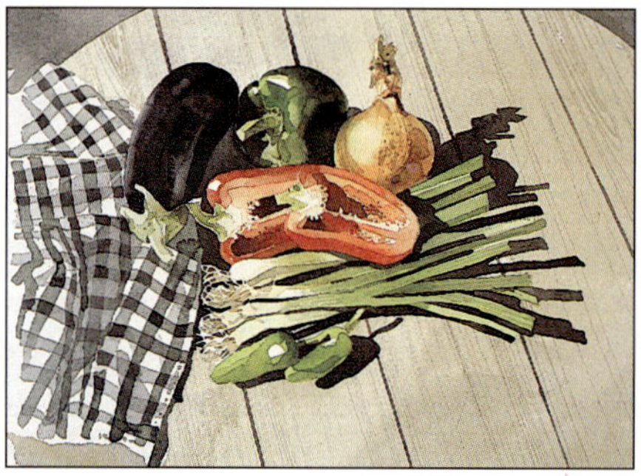

14 The finished picture.

Alternative Approaches

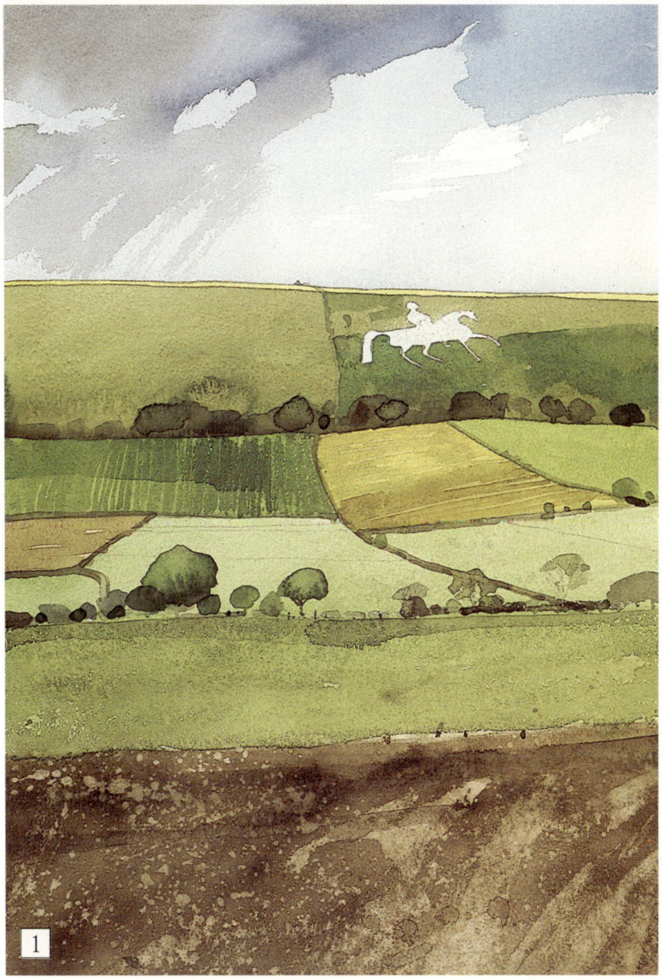

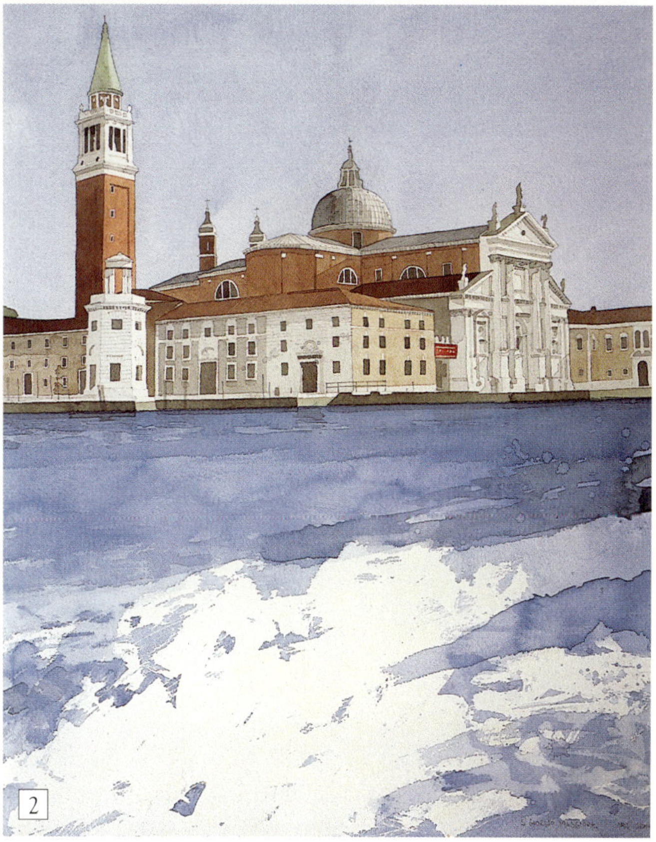

1 A range of techniques have been used to depict this white horse and rider carved into the hillside in Dorset. The area of the limestone figure was masked out with fluid and initial blocking-in worked wet into wet. Once dry, the fields were repainted, working wet on dry with plenty of gum arabic added. A wax candle was repeatedly used between washes as a resist to repel the paint and make interesting textural effects in what would otherwise have been a flat area of colour.

2 Prior to applying any paint, a large bristle oil painting brush was used to scrub on masking fluid across the area of water, giving a lively foreground to this painting of San Giorgio Maggiore in Venice.

ANEMONES

Using Gum Arabic

PROJECT THREE

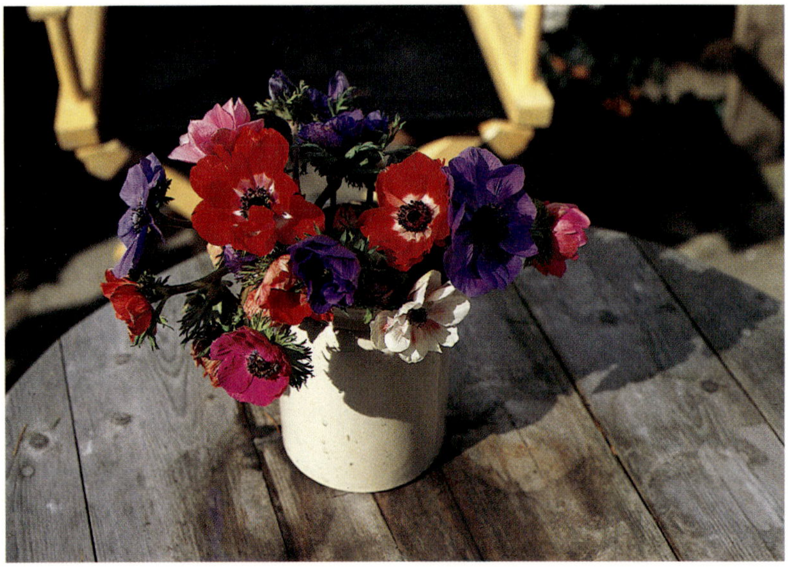

FLOWERS HAVE LONG BEEN A FAVOURED subject for the artist, be it as part of a large still life group or as a subject in their own right. They are easily obtained and the range and intensity of colour and their complexity of shape offer a very real challenge and endless picture-making possibilities. Flowers are not easy to paint well; a common mistake is to make the subject look too complex and over-arranged, with too wide a variety of colour and shape. Stick to simple, natural looking groups containing similar colours or species. In order to capture the precise shape and clarity of colour these anemones were worked using wet on dry washes: each layer of colour was allowed to dry before the next was glazed over the top.

The painting of the actual flowers may, at first sight, look dauntingly complicated, but the effect is achieved by using only three carefully painted layers, or washes, of paint – each layer of paint separates the subject into light, medium and dark tones. If you feel a tone or colour is too light or dark it can always be blotted off while still wet with a clean paper towel. Do not rub the mistake or the painted area will be smudged: simply dab the tissue hard on the area and lift off the colour.

The preliminary blocking in of the lightest tones was done with paint mixed only with water, but the later paint layers were mixed with gum arabic to increase the transparency of the paint while retaining the strength of colour. The addition of the gum arabic also means that the paint remains soluble when it is dry, so hard edges can be softened and colour lifted out simply by rewetting it. The simple neutral colours of the plain background, table top and pot help concentrate attention onto the bright colours of the anemones' arrangement.

There are, of course, several ways to approach the subject. An alternative would have been to work in reverse, masking out the colourful flowers with masking fluid, then working the background and table top before removing the masking fluid and working on the flowers.

MATERIALS AND EQUIPMENT

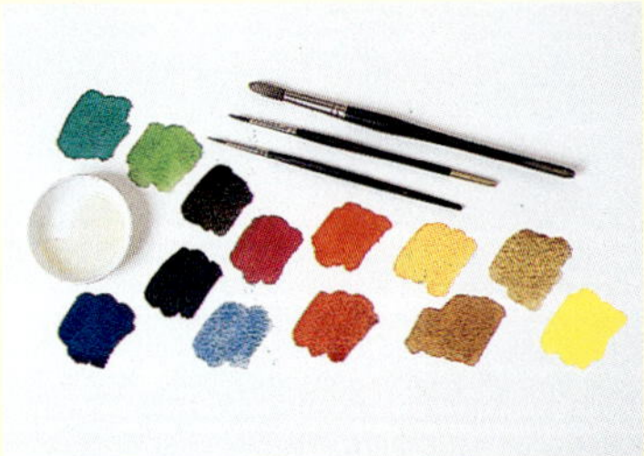

- 18x12in sheet of 300lb (638gsm) unstretched CP Waterford paper
- Three round brushes, no 12, no 5 and no 2
- Gum arabic
- Watercolours in the following colours: viridian, sap green, ivory black, Payne's gray, Antwerp blue, alizarin crimson, cerulean blue, cadmium red, brown madder alizarin, yellow ochre, burnt umber, raw umber and lemon yellow

The Painting

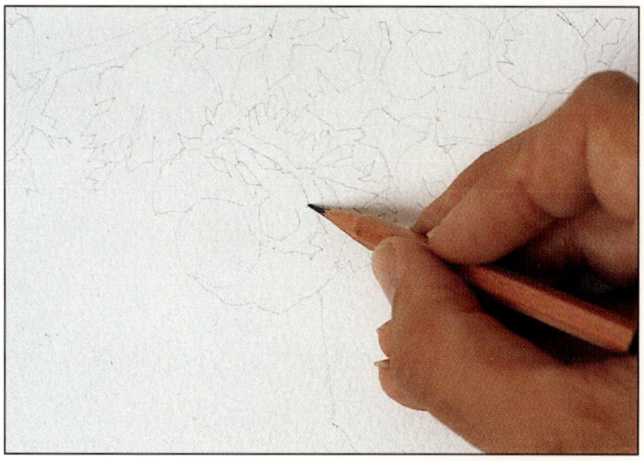

1 A detailed pencil drawing in a light HB pencil establishes the basic shape of the flowers and the jar, and helps keep the painting on track. Do not press too hard or the pencil line may show through the lighter colours.

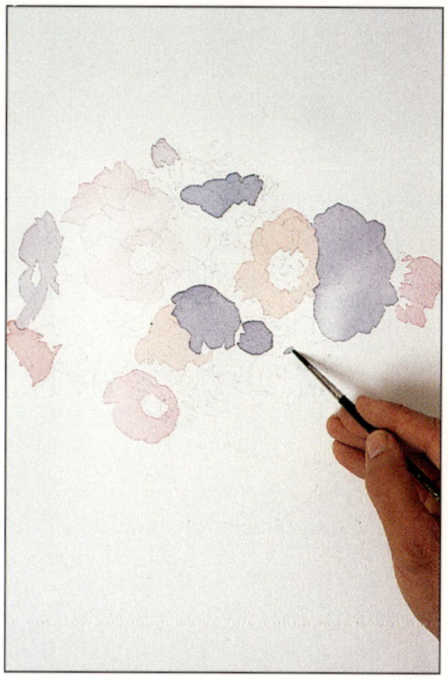

2 Using the no 5 round brush, the lightest tones found on each flower are laid in using a mix of alizarin crimson and Antwerp blue for the purple flowers and mixes of alizarin crimson and cadmium red for the pink and red flowers. Ivory black and a little lemon yellow give the light grey seen on the white flower at the front. To prevent colours running together make sure one colour is dry before painting another next to it.

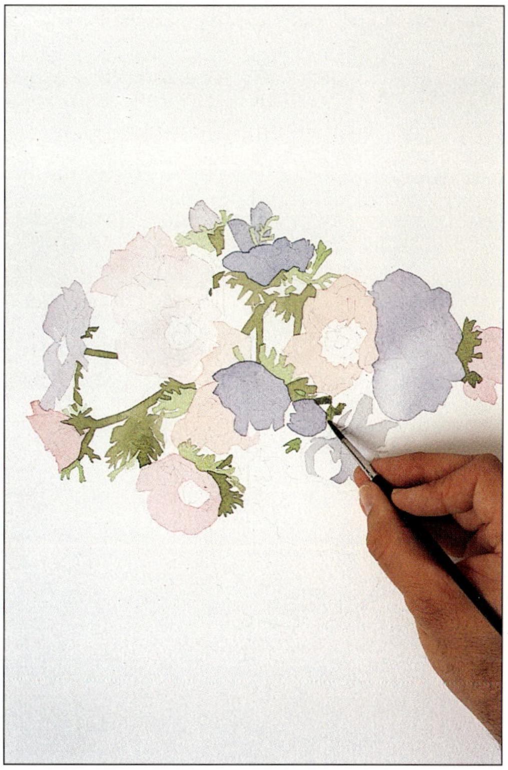

3 Once the flowers have dried, with a pale green – made from viridian and lemon yellow – paint in the palest leaves, darken the colour with sap green and a little brown madder alizarin and complete the rest of the foliage. Follow your drawing carefully and keep the angular shape of the leaves crisp and sharp.

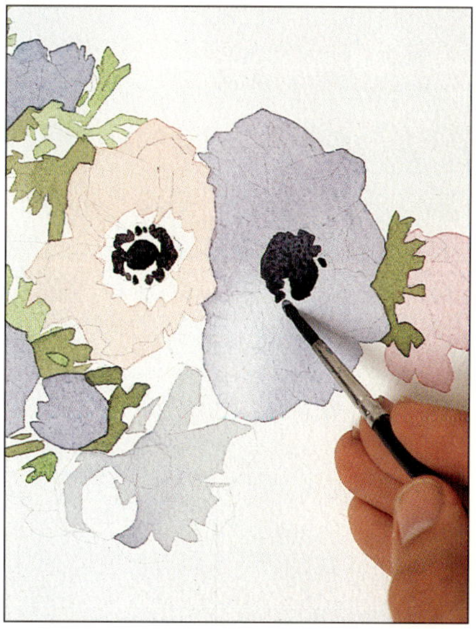

4 Ivory black, Payne's gray, sap green and alizarin crimson mixes give the range of dark colours that are found in the flower centres.

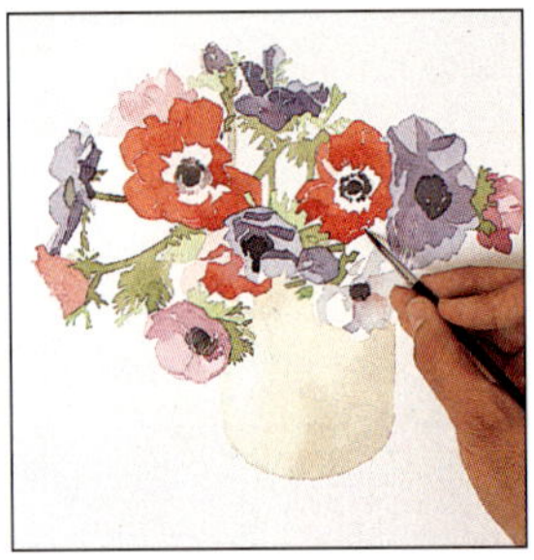

5 A light mix of yellow ochre and burnt umber establishes the colour of the pot. For the shadow, this mix is darkened with more umber and worked down the side wet into wet. Then, working slowly and keeping the colours separate, the mid tones on each flower head are painted; add a little gum arabic into each mix to intensify the colours. Antwerp blue and alizarin crimson are used for the purple flowers, cadmium red dulled with brown madder alizarin for the red flowers and alizarin crimson and cerulean blue for the pink flowers. The white flower is wet with clean water and a little red flower mix is touched in to give the slight red tinge seen on the petals.

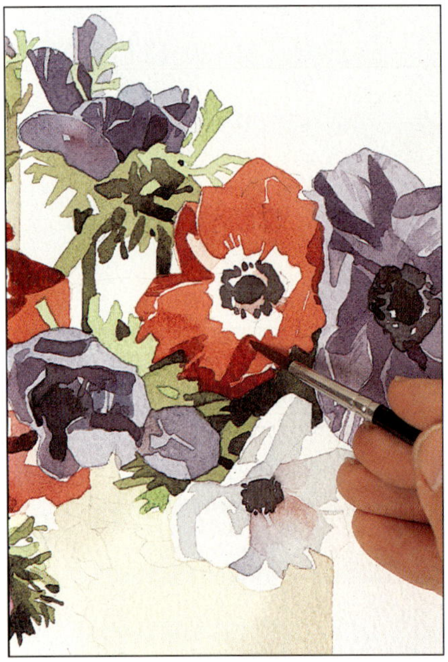

6 Still using the no 5 round brush, the dark leaves and petals are painted with sap green darkened with brown madder alizarin and Payne's gray.

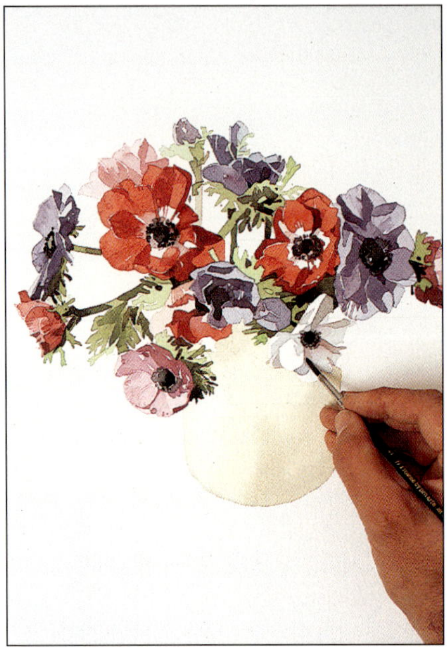

7 All of the flower mixes are then darkened by strengthening the colour and the darkest tones added.

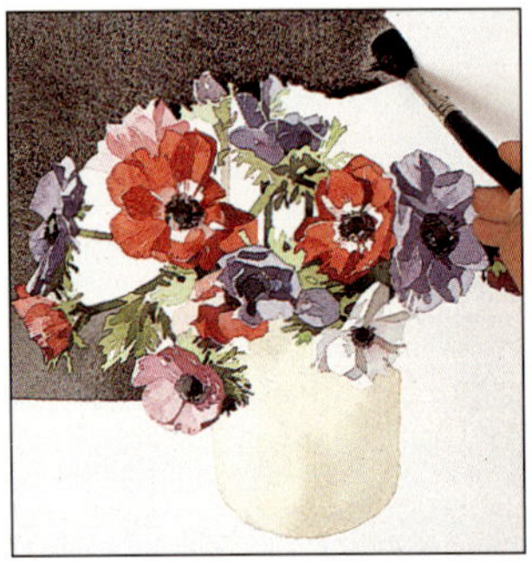

8 The background is painted in one coat with burnt umber darkened with Payne's gray; make sure that you have enough paint mixed to cover the whole area. Using the no 12 round brush, work quickly across the paper painting as close to the flower heads as the large brush will allow. Switch to a smaller brush when working tight up to the intricate shapes made by the flowers.

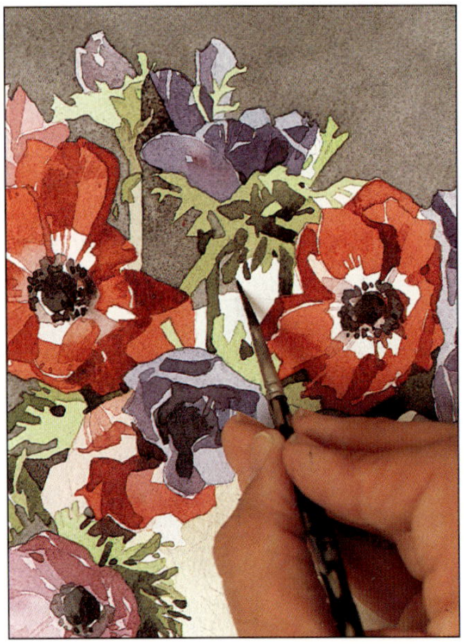

9 The no 2 round brush is then used to paint the negative shapes that are found in and around the flower heads and leaves.

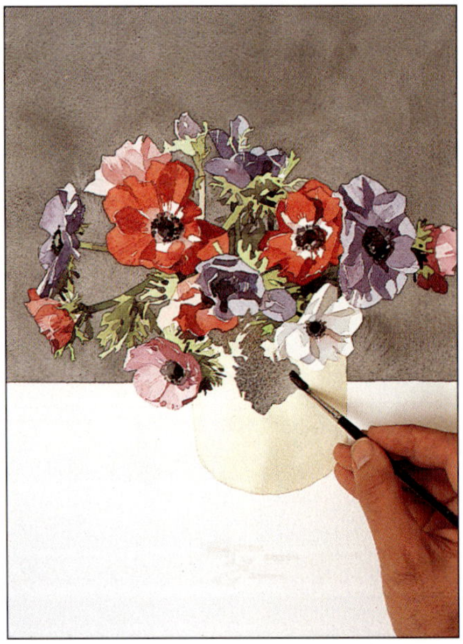

10 Add a little antwerp blue and gum arabic to the background colour and with the no 5 round brush block in the shadow cast by the flowers onto the pot.

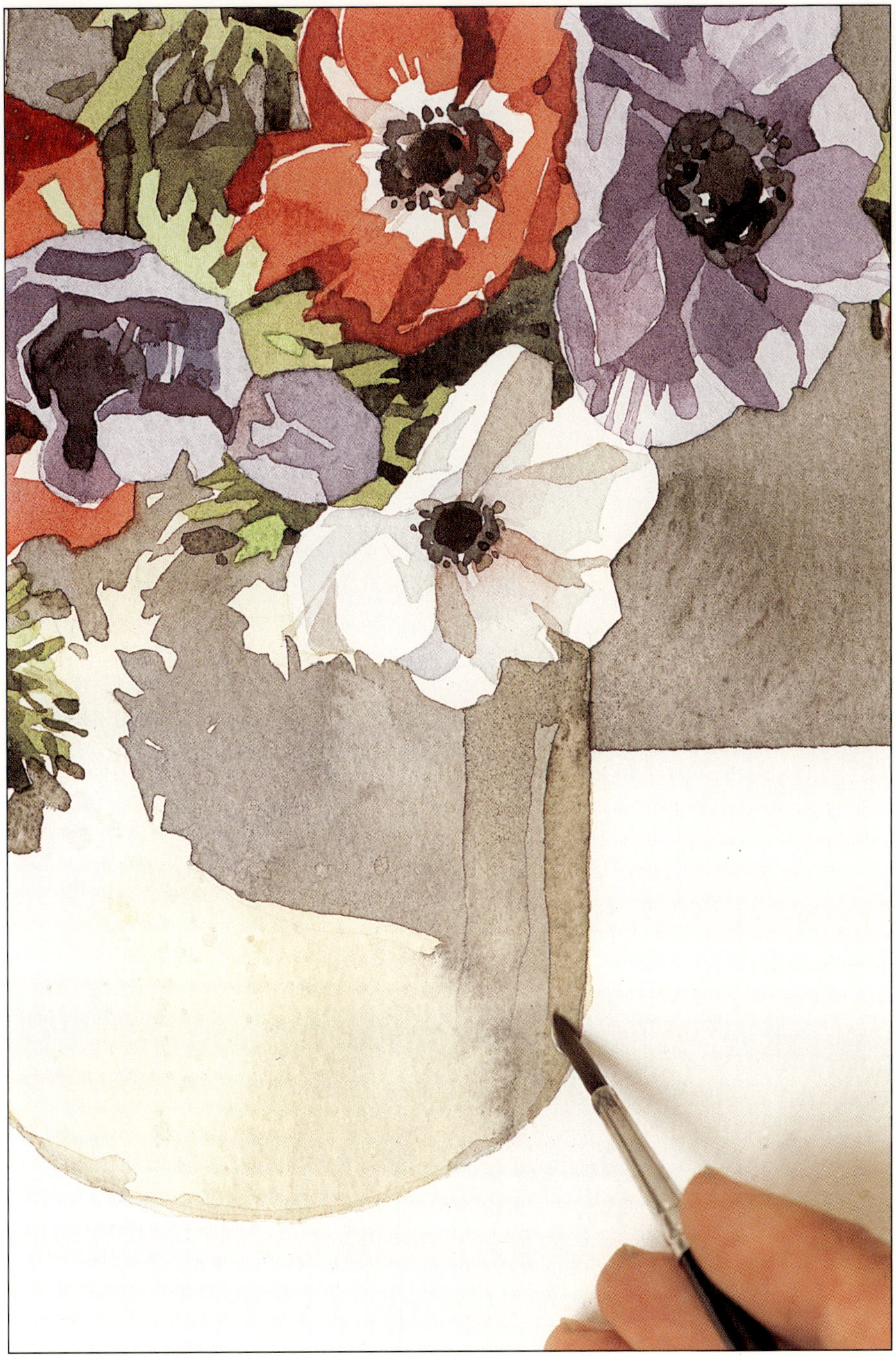

11 Allow this to dry and with clean water brush in two marks that give a suggestion of a reflection in the glaze of the jar. Then establish the colour of the table top with a raw umber and Payne's gray mix

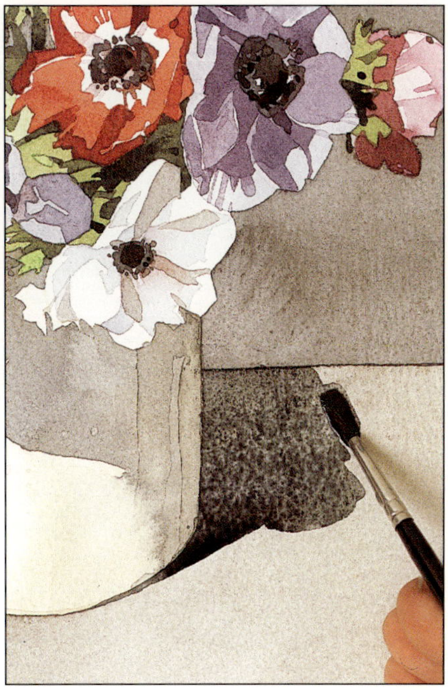

12 Payne's gray with the addition of a little Antwerp blue gives a coolish colour for the shadow thrown onto and across the table by the pot.

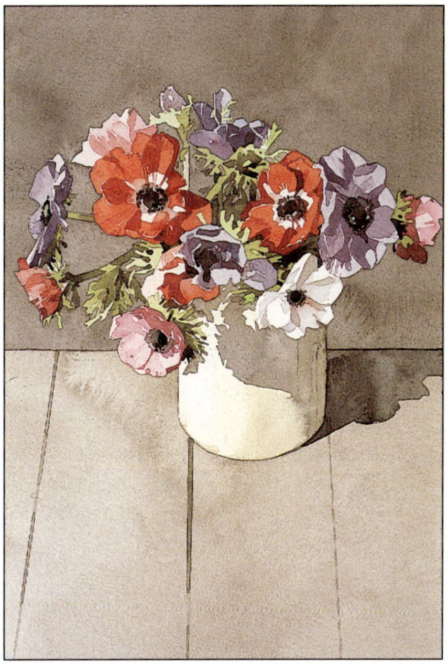

13 A ruler helps with painting in the straight lines of the wood using a grey and umber mix.

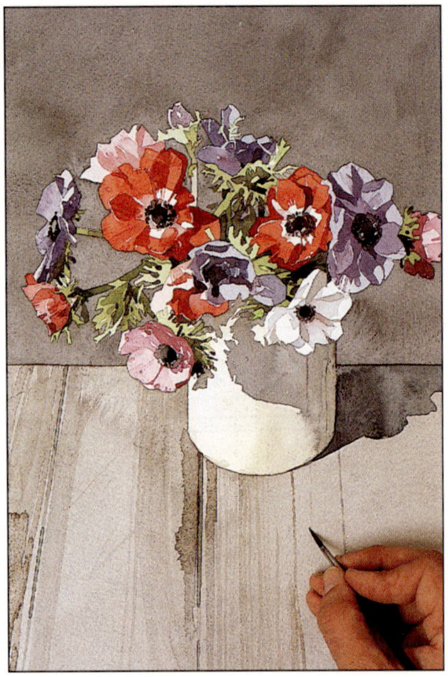

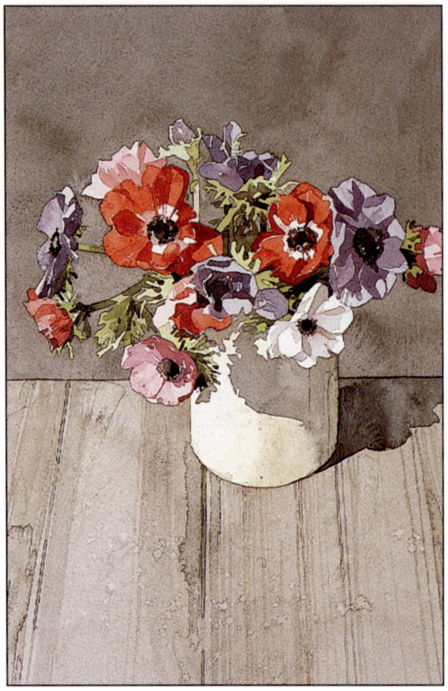

14 The grain of the wood is then painted in free-hand with the no 5 round brush.

15 The painting is finished by spattering the table top and jar with clean water; this dries leaving a watermark that gives a weathered look to the table.

Alternative Approaches

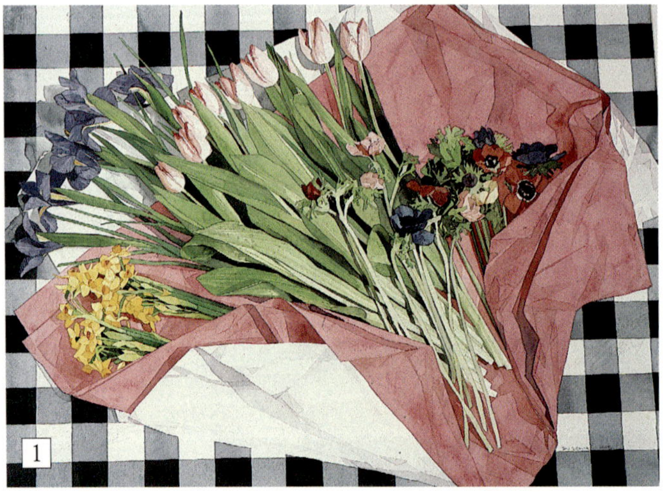

1 Rather than showing flowers as they are more usually seen – arranged in a vase – this painting shows them strewn onto a table top having been just unwrapped. The painting, while being complex, is very structured. Each species of flower lies grouped together and the whole arrangement is kept in order by the mauve tissue paper that runs diagonally, cutting across the vertical and horizontal bands of the table cloth.

2 The painting of parrot tulips (opposite) is painted in a looser style; the shape of the pattern describes the shape of the tulips. The leaves were painted using a combination of wet on dry and wet in wet, so that some of the leaves remain defined while others blend together. The shadow was painted in two washes: the first, describing the shadow of the window frame, was allowed to dry slightly before painting in the darker shadow thrown from the tulips and the stool.

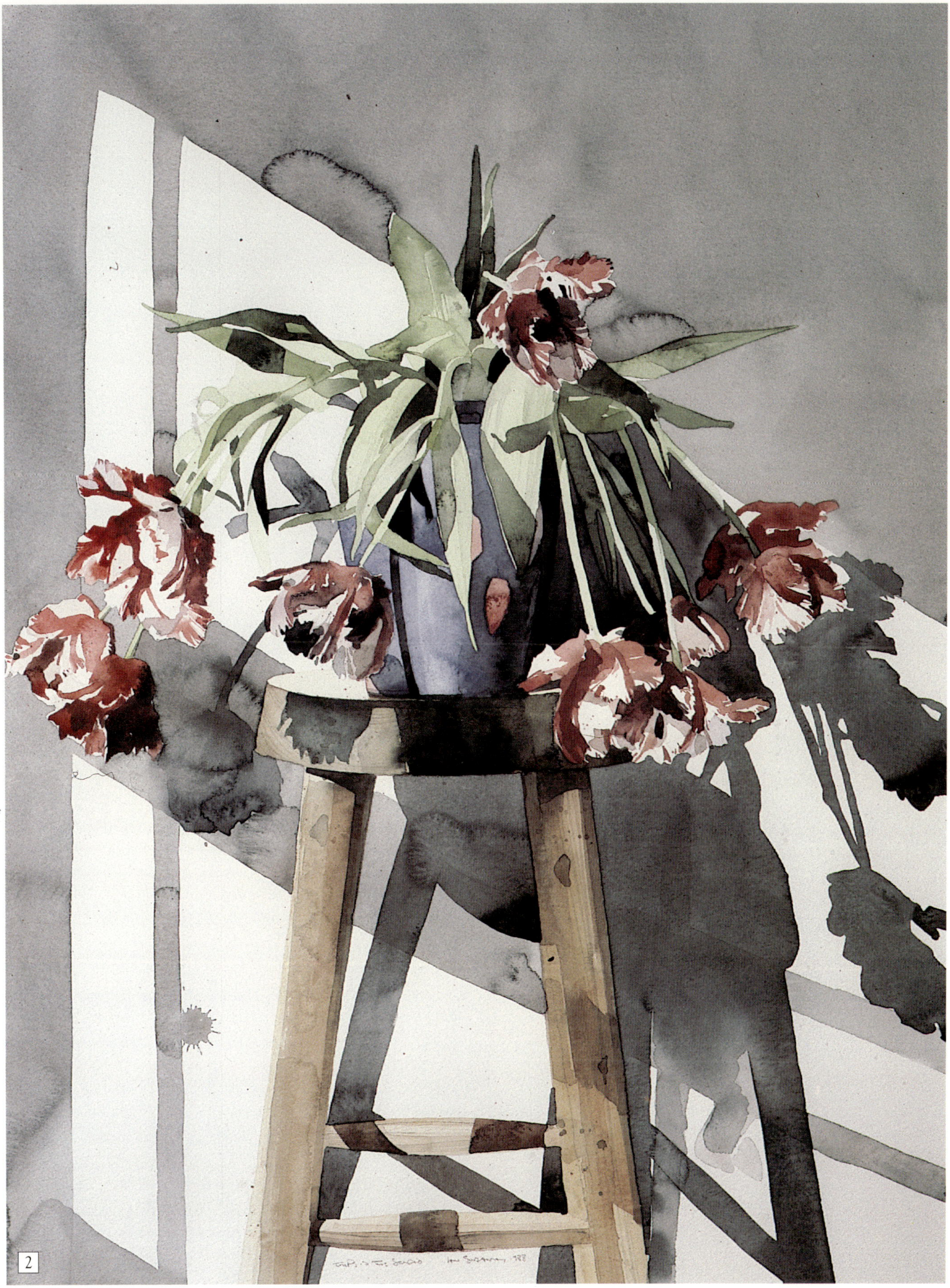

2

CRAB AND LANGOUSTINE

Creating Texture

PROJECT FOUR

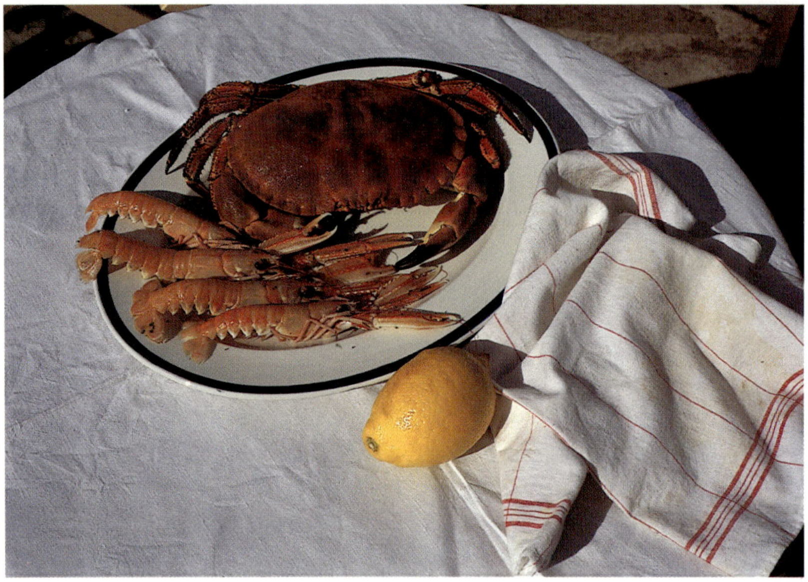

INTRODUCING marks into a painting that would be difficult, if not impossible, to make with a brush can be very liberating, opening up all manner of possibilities. In life the range of textures and patterns that are an intrinsic part of things is vast and varied. Grass, wood, stone, materials and fabrics, water – everywhere we look surfaces shout for special treatment. The problem is usually solved with expressive brushwork: flicks, dabs, blobs, strokes and dots, all executed with the trusty brush.

While it is true that the range of brush shapes and types are capable of laying down paint in a wide variety of ways, and that experience has shown that they are generally the best tool for the job, they are by their very nature limited, and not necessarily the only tool that can be used. Becoming skilled with a brush takes time, and results that are occasionally better and more convincing – and often very quick to do – can be achieved in a number of alternative ways, none of which compromise the look or feel of an otherwise traditionally painted picture.

Sponges have long been thought of as an essential addition to the watercolour artist's equipment, used as they are for wetting paper prior to stretching, for applying a wash and lifting out colour, or for making corrections. They are also capable of solving a range of complex mark-making problems in a very simple and straightforward way. Dipped into paint and stippled over the paper surface, a complex mottled pattern can be achieved. This can be allowed to dry and then worked over using traditional washes or reworked with the sponge, using a similar or different colour to build up a multi-layered textural effect. The same technique can be employed using clean water and a brush full of paint. The brush then only needs to be touched to the wet surface for the paint to flow into the shape left by the wet sponge. This technique can be used in very small areas and with intricate shapes if a mask is used.

In this painting of seafood, a cut card was also employed to paint in the creases and shadows on the tablecloth, and while a very similar effect could have been achieved with a brush, the paint did lie on the paper in a different way. The effect was also achieved with speed and a certain satisfying economy, which is always an advantage.

MATERIALS AND EQUIPMENT

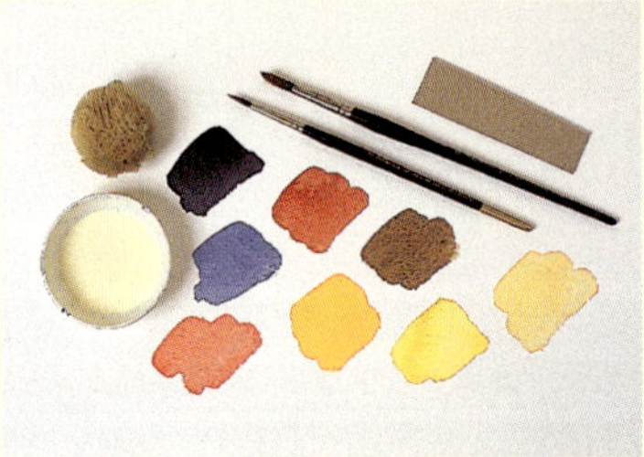

- 13x14in sheet of stretched 200lb (425gsm) CP Bockingford watercolour paper
- Piece of thick card cut into a chisel shape
- Two round brushes, no 8 and no 5
- Small natural sponge
- Masking fluid
- Watercolours in the following colours: Payne's gray, cobalt blue, cadmium red, brown madder, alizarin, cadmium yellow, burnt umber, lemon yellow and Naples yellow

The Painting

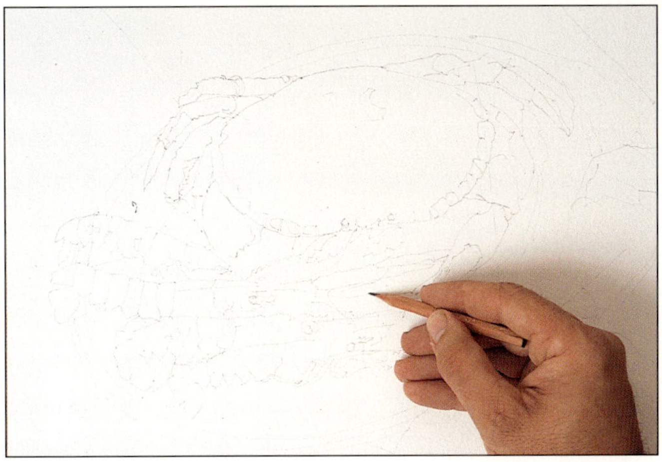

1 A light HB-pencil drawing helps position the crab and langoustine; the format is almost square, with the plate sitting diagonally across the paper. The darkish mass of the seafood at the top of the picture is balanced by the napkin running off the edge and the bright yellow of the lemon next to it.

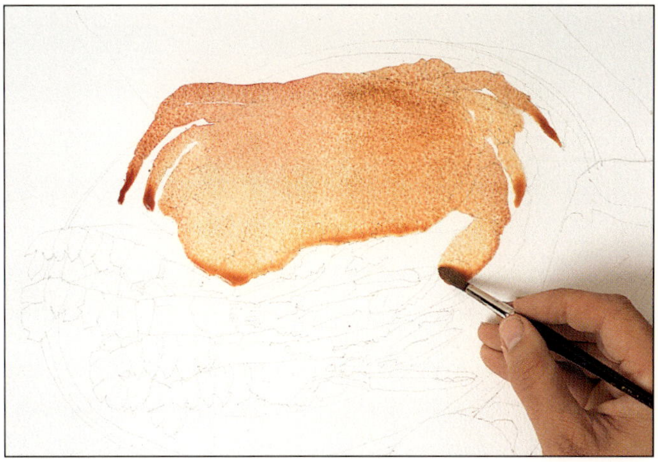

2 Mix three washes consisting of the following colours: cadmium red, burnt umber and cadmium yellow; cadmium red, brown madder alizarin and cadmium yellow; cadmium red and Naples yellow. Using the no 8 round brush, paint in the darkest mix (cadmium red, burnt umber and cadmium yellow), working around the crab legs and the back of its shell.

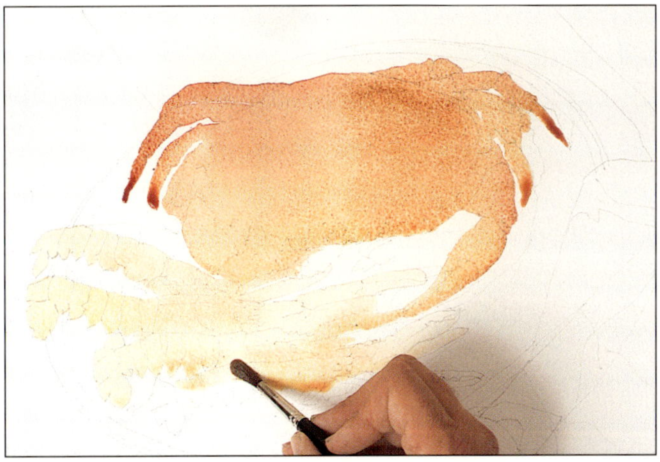

3 Work across the middle of the shell using the slightly lighter mix (cadmium red, brown madder alizarin and cadmium yellow) and finally establish the overall colour of the langoustine using the mix of cadmium red and Naples yellow.

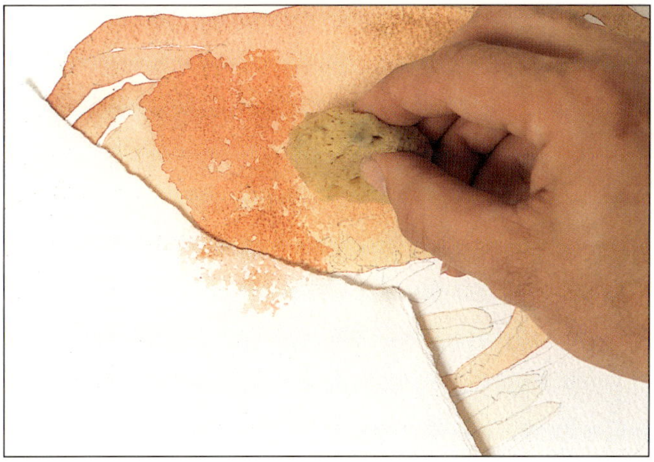

4 Tear a piece of medium-weight watercolour paper to give an edge that has a slight curve. Use this as a mask to prevent paint getting onto those areas where it is not wanted. With the small sponge, or a piece cut from a larger one, dab on some texture over the crab shell to resemble the rough, pitted surface. Next, use the darkest mix from the previous step and, darkened with a little more brown madder alizarin and a little more burnt umber, dab across the surface of the shell to describe the rough, pitted surface.

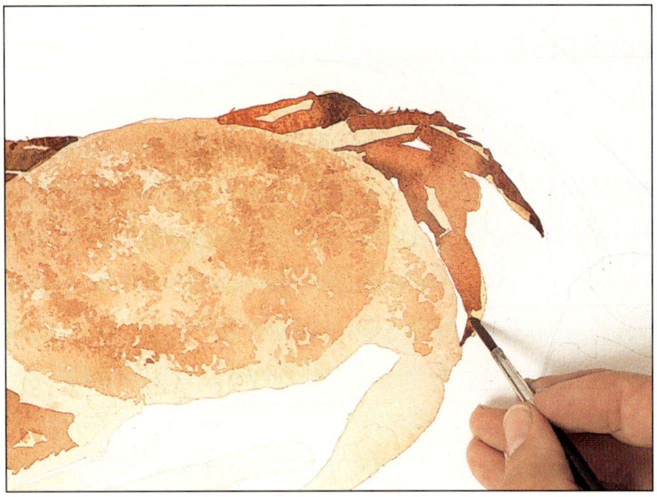

5 Allow the sponged texture to dry and repeat the process to give a layered effect. Using the no 5 round brush and a dark, rich mix of brown madder alizarin, Payne's gray and cadmium yellow, paint in the dark areas of the legs and claws, cutting in carefully to preserve the distinctive edge of the shell.

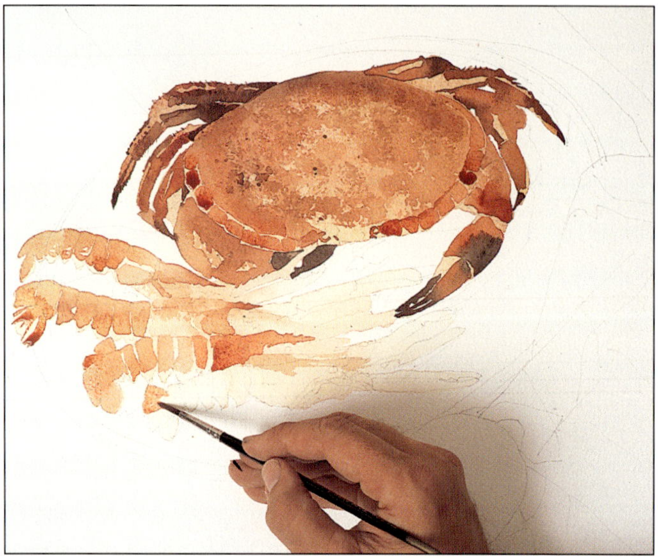

6 Add more Payne's gray and burnt umber for the dark colour at the end of the claws, then lighten the mixture with water and, looking carefully, describe the segmented langoustine shells. Add a little Naples yellow to the very light shell colour and paint in the pinkish shadows that can be seen on the plate.

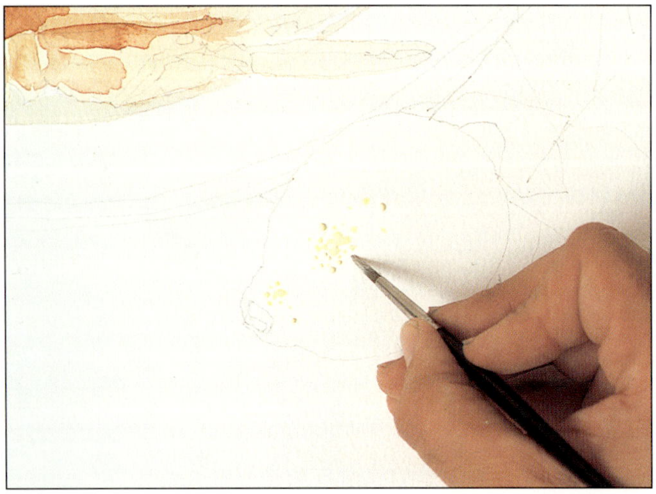

7 The light reflections on the pitted surface of the lemon are reproduced by dotting on a little masking fluid using an old brush.

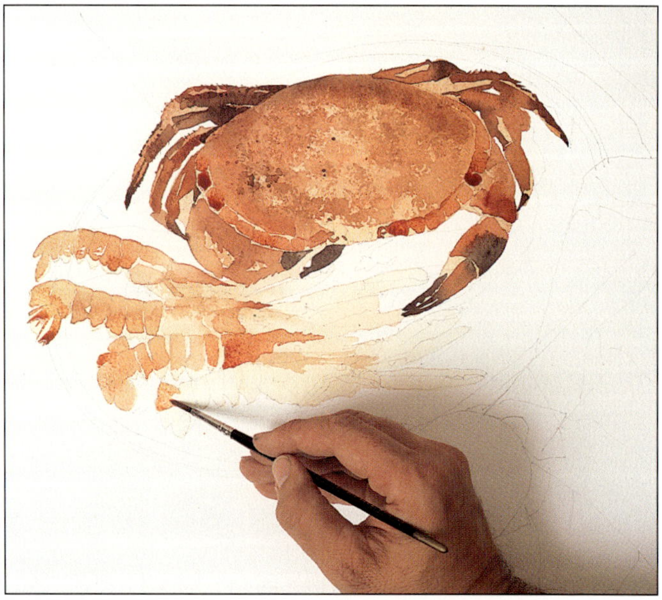

8 Colour some clean water with Payne's gray and cobalt blue and, using the no 8 round brush, wash over the white table cloth, working around the plate. Darken the mix used for the crab shell with burnt umber, brown madder alizarin and Payne's gray, then wet the shell area by dabbing on water with the sponge and touch in the dark paint around its edges; the mix will run into the wet area finding its own place to rest.

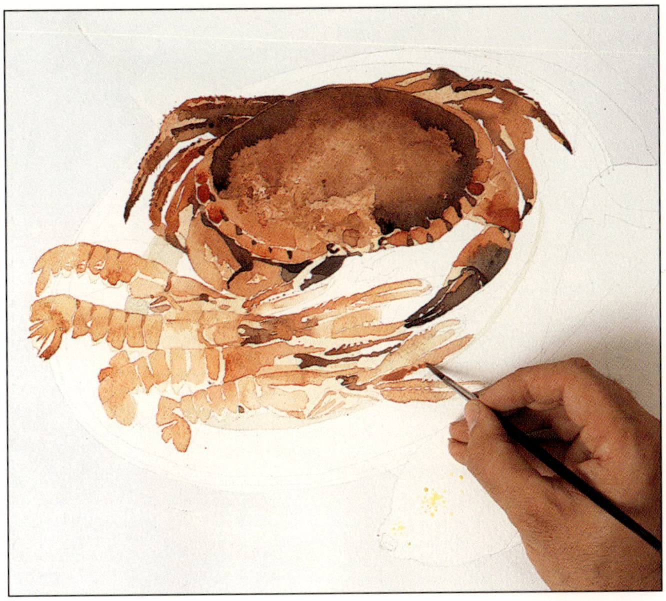

9 Using the same mix and the no 5 round brush, paint the shadows seen in the crevices around the shell edge, the eyes and the spiky fine hairs on the legs. Finally, darken and paint in the detail on the claws by adding a little more Payne's gray into the mix.

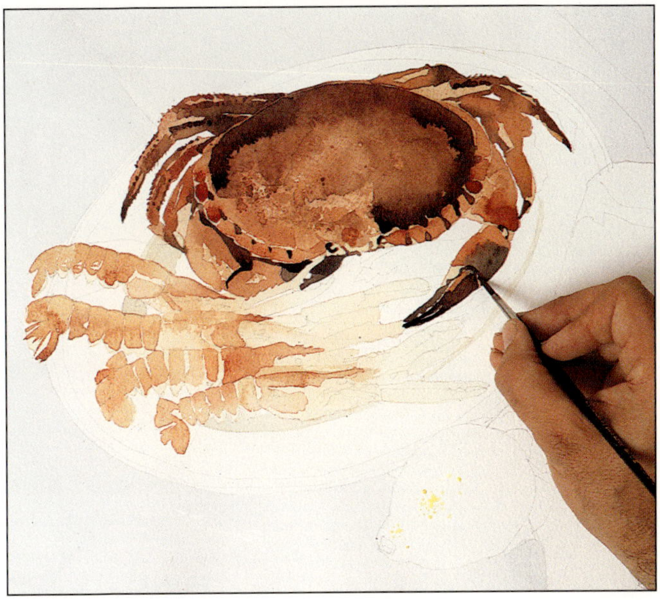

10 Lighten these mixes a little with water and, still using the no 5 round brush, sharpen the segments on the langoustine and bring in some detail to their heads and claws.

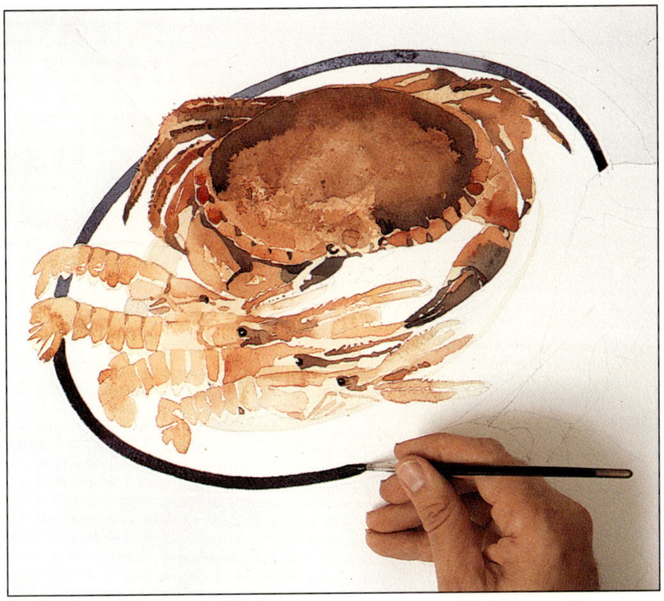

11 Cobalt blue added to Payne's gray gives the colour for the blue line around the edge of the plate. This helps define the plate area and separates it from the light tablecloth, visually lifting the seafood. The lemon is blocked in using a cadmium yellow and lemon yellow mix.

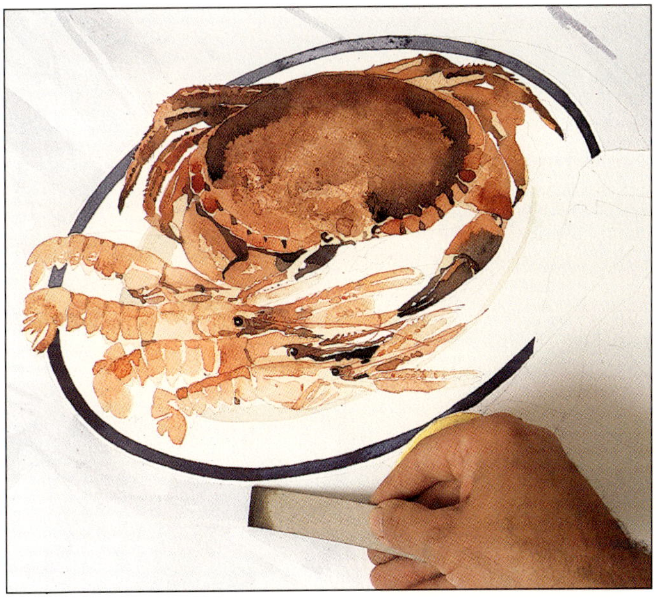

12 Payne's gray and cobalt blue also give a light grey for the shadows and creases found on the white table cloth. Dip the end of the chisel-shaped piece of thick card into the mix and use it to paint on the creases and shadows. By altering the angle of the card the shape of the mark will vary; a very thin line can be obtained by using the card on its edge.

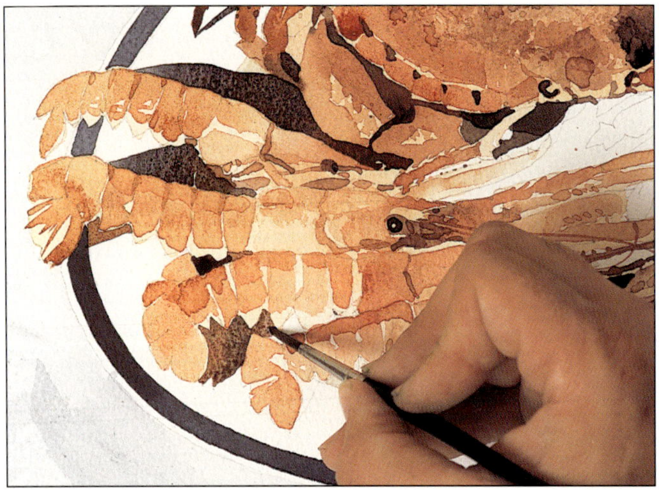

13 Varying mixes of Payne's gray and brown madder alizarin will give the blue-brown colours found in the shadows beneath and around the crab and langoustine.

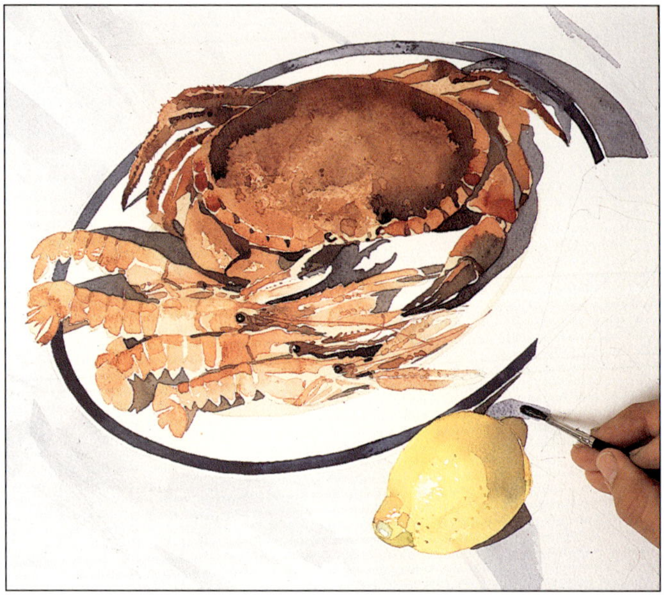

14 The painting is completed by finishing the lemon with a little cobalt blue mixed with lemon yellow for the green, and a light wash of Payne's gray for the shadow.

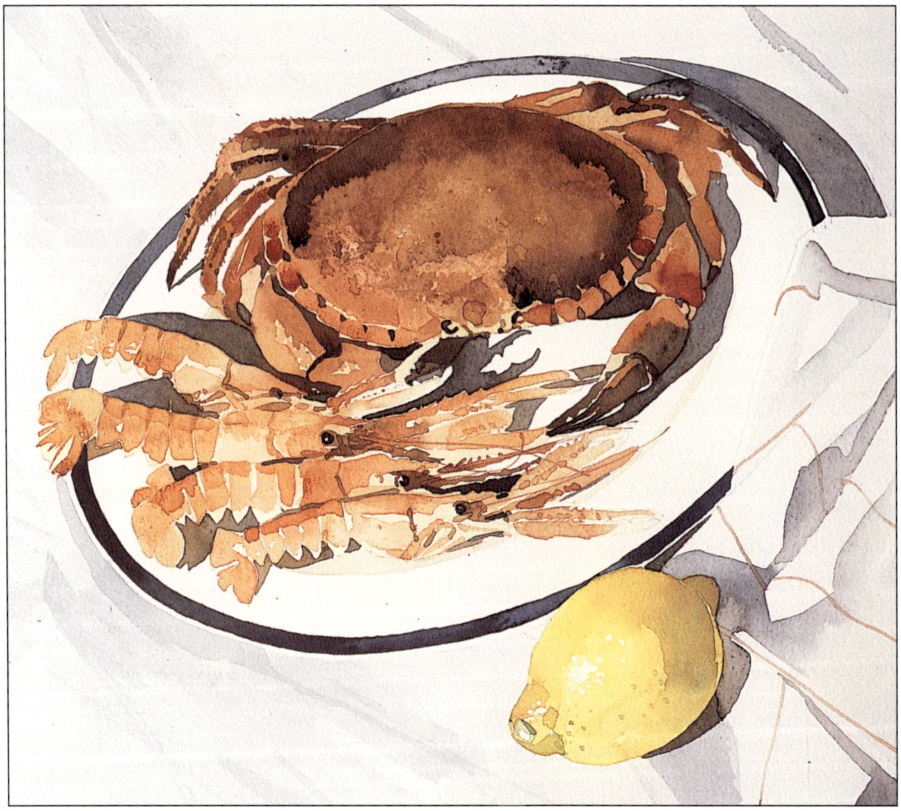

15 Once dry, the masking fluid is rubbed away to reveal the paper highlights. Payne's gray and brown madder alizarin are again used for the dark shadows on the cloth. Finally, the red pattern on the napkin is painted using brown madder alizarin.

Alternative Approaches

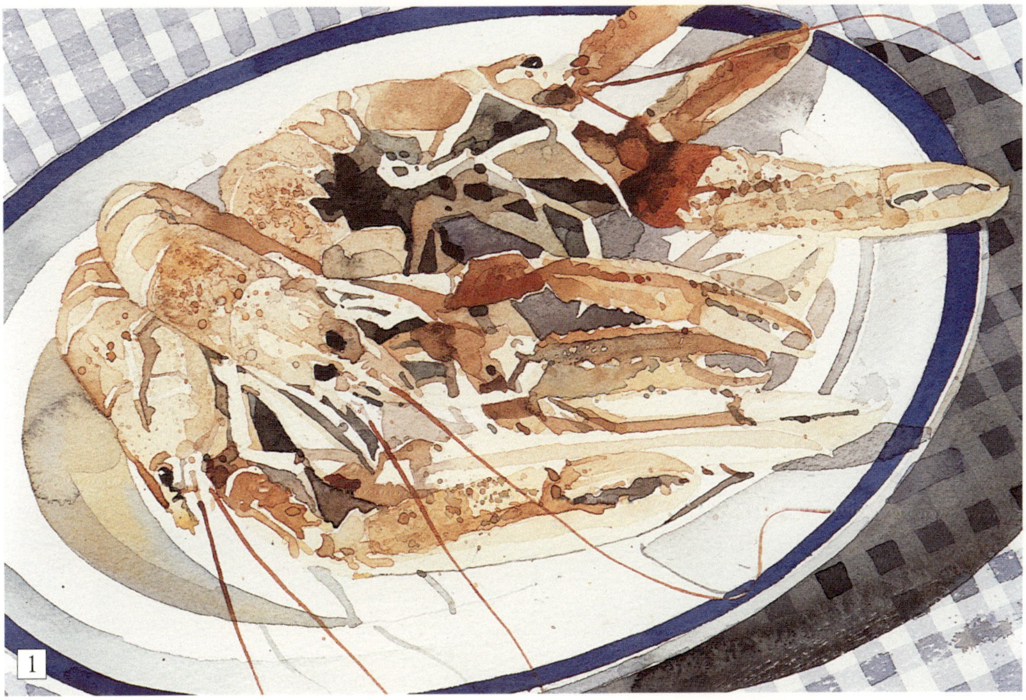

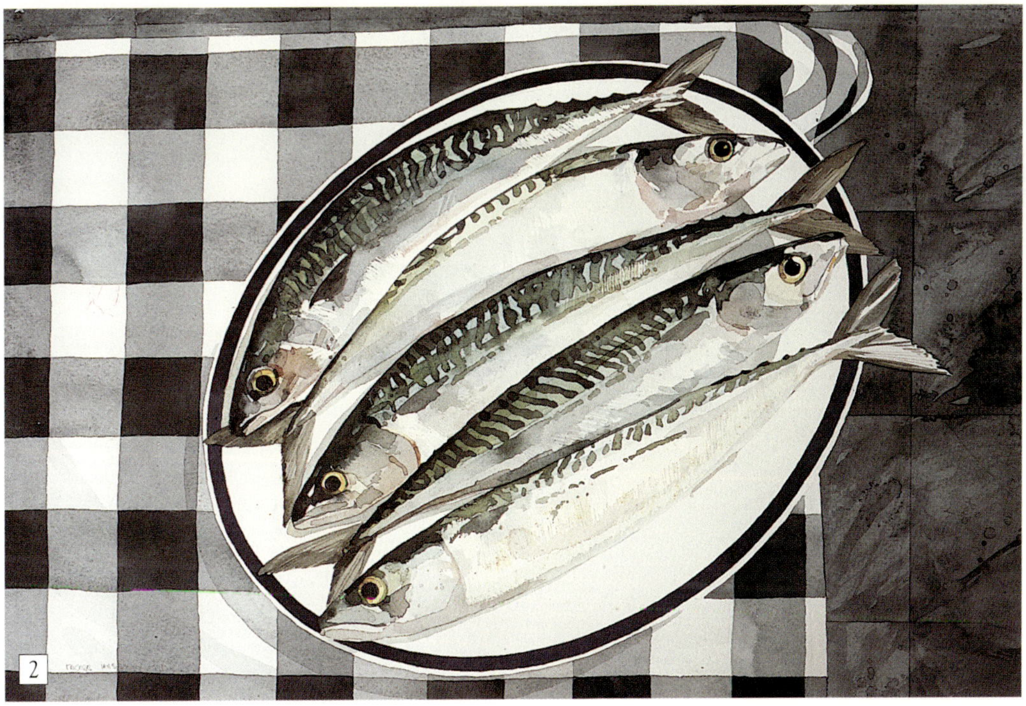

1 This plate of langoustine has been made to fill the picture area. The blue edge of the plate confines the subject and makes a closed composition. The shells have been spattered just enough to suggest some pattern and texture.

2 In this painting the mackerel are made to look silvery and wet by simply drawing the patterns of reflected light seen on the scales with a fine-nibbed drawing pen dipped in masking fluid. Plenty of gum arabic was used in the mixes to keep the paint bright, light and transparent.

BOATS ON A BEACH

Masking and Spattering

PROJECT FIVE

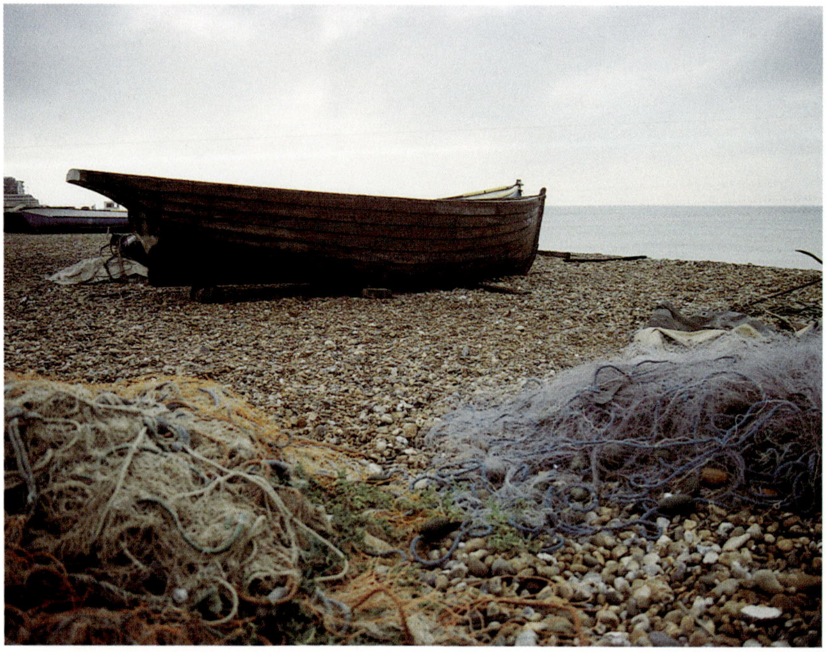

WITH CAREFUL and painstaking observation, and with a certain degree of skill, it is possible to recreate the scene before you with complete precision; however the result can be less than satisfactory. The slow process of representing each and every detail can make the picture look dull and uninspired, regardless of the skill that it took to paint it. The problem may sometimes be one of simply overworking or taking things too far; having successfully accomplished what was intended the artist adds a touch here and a touch there, and before long the spark is lost.

Do remember that a complicated-looking subject can often be painted more convincingly and retain greater visual interest if it is treated with a certain amount of artistic or creative licence. Many purists frown on using anything other than traditional brush techniques, but I believe that artists, by definition, are inquisitive and inventive folk, who should use whatever is to hand in order to solve tricky problems of representation.

The seashore is a grand place to work, and boats are grand and challenging subjects to paint. They are often very colourful or, if not, like our subject they are beaten and weathered from years of hard work and standing up to the elements. At a glance the view offers little to work with, but by making a few decisions early on about possible treatments the options begin to widen and grow.

The beach and the pile of old nets are a challenge as both are visually highly complex. In the painting, the beach was spattered with paint to give the impression of millions of multi-coloured pebbles. By allowing each colour to dry before spattering another, the tiny blobs of colour dry separately. The illusion is carried further by painting the pebbles larger the nearer they get to the forefront of the painting. Masking the area with torn paper accomplishes two things: it keeps the rest of the painting clean, and the rough, uneven edge gives a distinct quality to the edge of the masked area. The same is true of the tape used to carve out the shape of the pile of nets. These presented their own set of problems, so a loose impression of what was there was considered to be the best solution.

MATERIALS AND EQUIPMENT

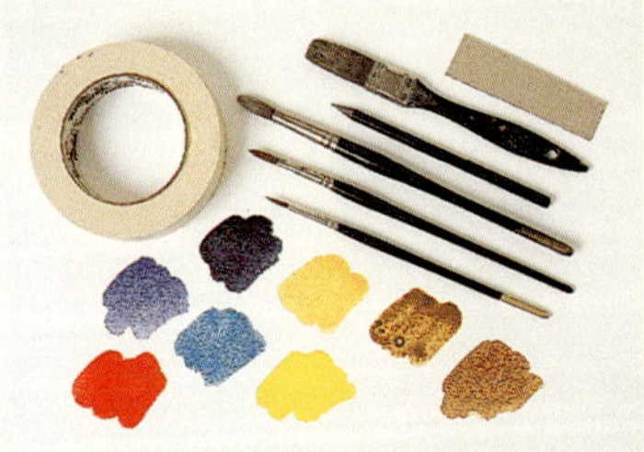

- 15x22in sheet of stretched 200lb (425gsm) CP Bockingford watercolour paper
- Thick piece of card
- Bristle oil painting or decorator's brush, 1in wide
- 2B graphite stick
- Three round brushes, no 12, no 8 and no 5
- Drafting tape
- Watercolours in the following colours: Payne's gray, cobalt blue, cadmium red, yellow ochre, cerulean blue, burnt umber, cadmium yellow and raw umber

The Painting

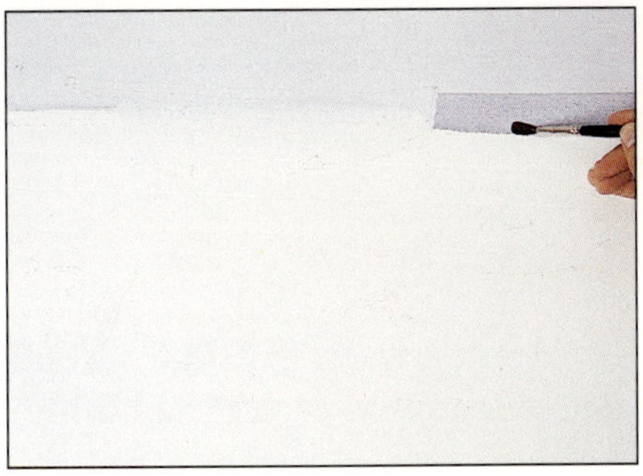

1 The boat, position of the horizon and the nets in the foreground can be established in light pencil if you wish. Using the no 8 round brush and a dilute mix of cobalt blue, apply a flat wash over the sky area down into the sea and across the boat; do not bring the wash down onto the beach. Once dry, darken the mix with Payne's gray and a little yellow ochre and, using the same brush, paint in the sea as a flat wash. Make sure the horizon line runs horizontal and is square to the side edge of the picture.

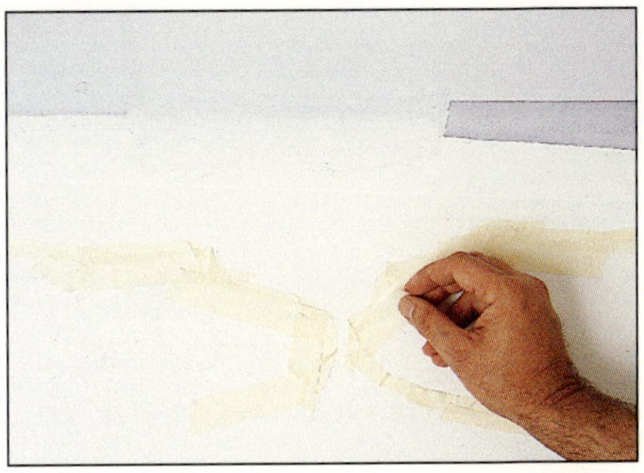

2 Apply drafting tape to approximate the shape of the piles of discarded fishing net. Do use drafting tape and not masking tape, as the latter is far stickier and may pull the surface off the paper when it is removed.

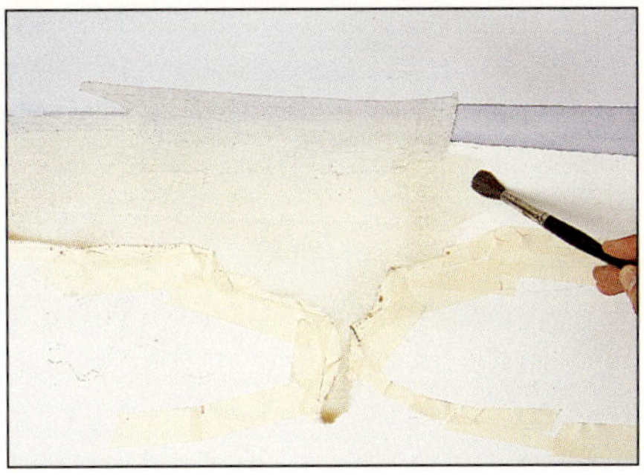

3 Mix a thin wash consisting of raw umber and yellow ochre. Using the no 12 round brush paint this across the area of beach and over the boats, paying particular attention to the edge that runs against the sky and the sea.

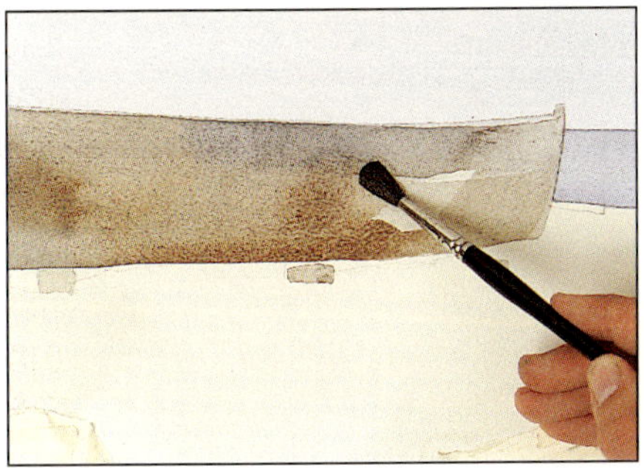

4 With a light mix of raw umber and cobalt blue, and using the same brush, paint in the boats. Allow the wash to dry, then darken the mix with burnt umber and Payne's gray and repaint, cutting out the shapes at the stern of the boat and leaving a pale edge along the top edge.

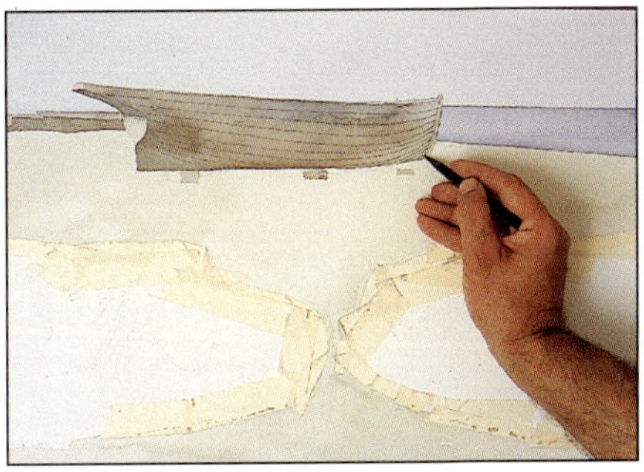

5 With the 2B graphite stick carefully draw in the shape and direction of the wooden planks on the boat.

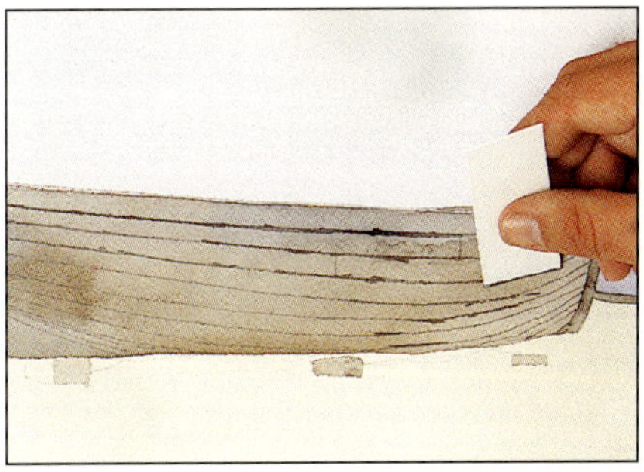

6 Using a thin piece of card dipped in a dark raw umber and Payne's gray mix, darken the shadows that run along beneath each plank.

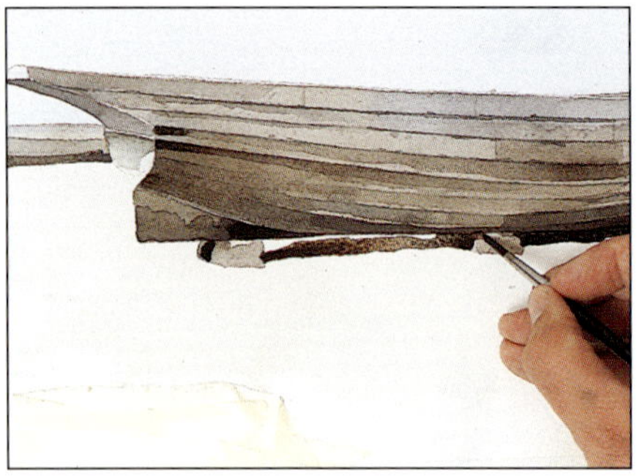

7 Intensify the mixture with a little more burnt umber; using the no 5 round brush, darken those planks that are in shadow around the belly of the boat and the area of shingle that lies directly beneath the boat.

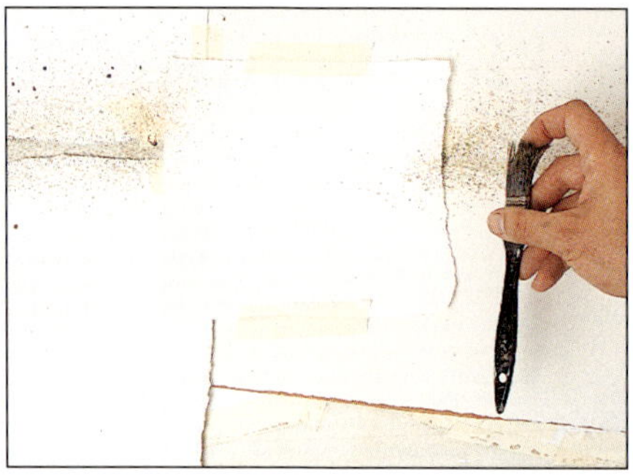

8 A band of shingle is spattered running across the middle of the picture. In order to do this the rest of the painting needs to be covered to prevent splashes of paint falling where they are not wanted. Medium-weight watercolour paper is torn to give an interesting line and secured into place with drafting tape. Different ochre and brown mixes are then spattered across the desired area using the 1-in bristle brush. Each mix is allowed to dry before spattering the next.

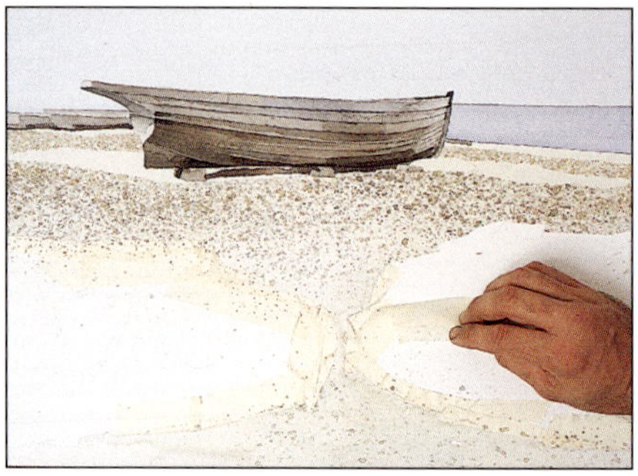

9 The paper mask is moved down a fraction and a second area is spattered across the bottom of the picture. Once the effect has been achieved the paper mask can be removed along with the drafting tape, leaving the shape of the nets.

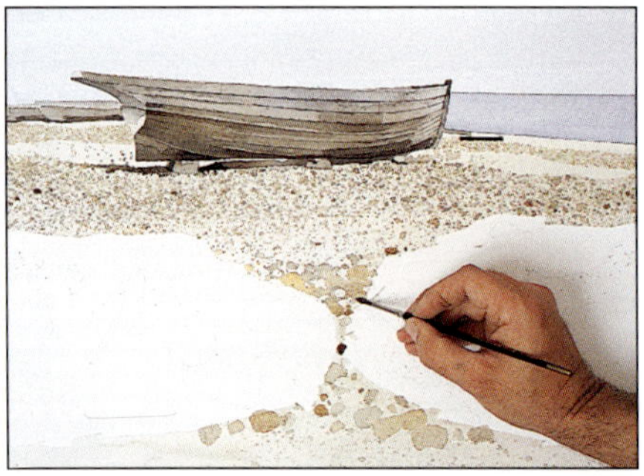

10 With a range of orange and brown mixes and using the no 5 round brush, paint in the shape of larger stones and pebbles.

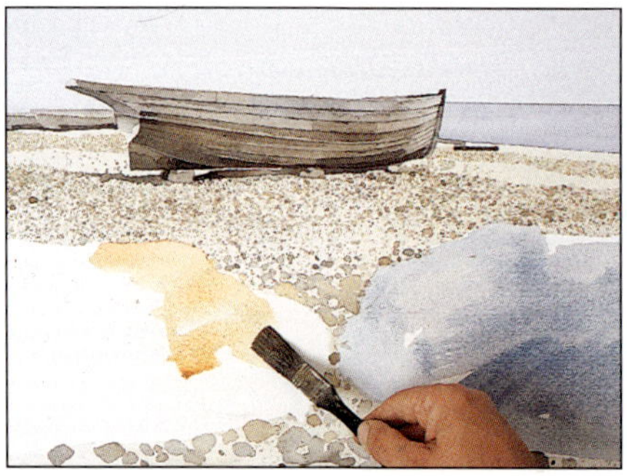

11 With the 1-in bristle brush loosely block in the nets using cerulean blue and a mix of cadmium red and cadmium yellow.

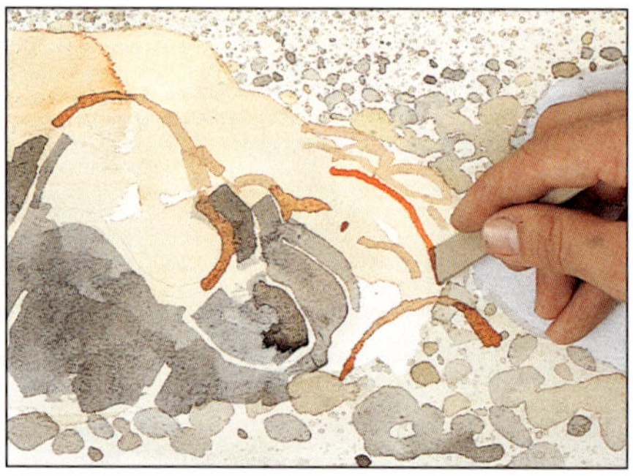

12 Using the piece of thick card and a range of browns and oranges mixed from the colours used previously, paint in the piles of discarded rope and netting, sometimes working the negative shapes. This allows the base colour to show through as strands of rope, while in other places the card is used to describe the bright orange of the tangled nylon nets.

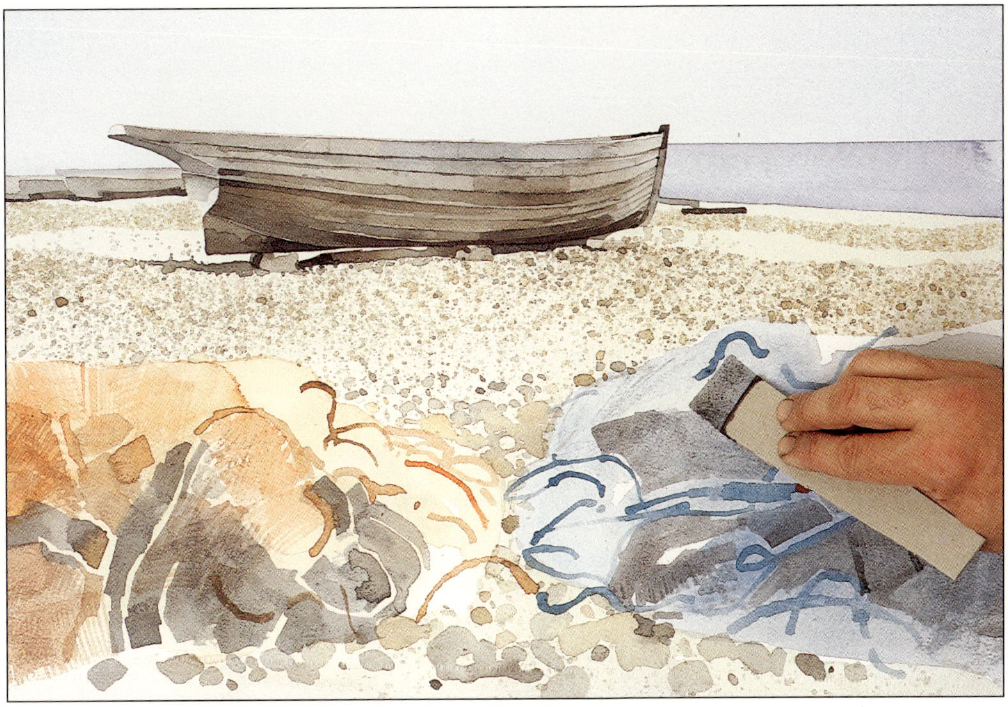

13 The no 5 round brush is used to paint in the finer net lines and the process is repeated with the blue. If and when the end of the card begins to deliver a messy line and becomes over-soggy, simply cut off the wet portion leaving a new crisp edge with which to work.

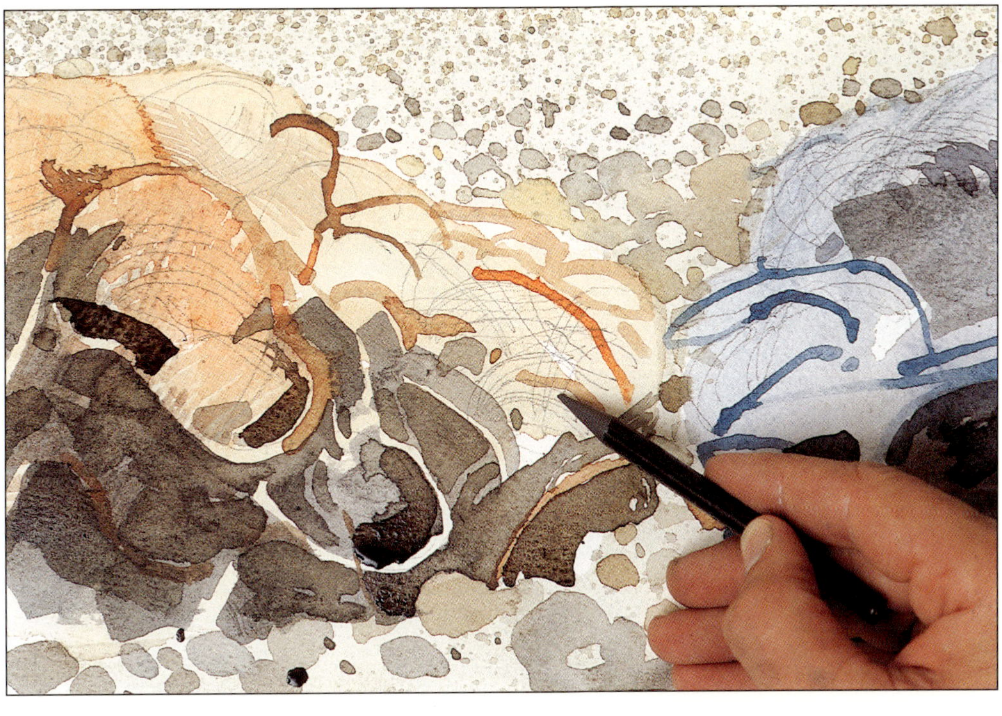

14 Finally, using the 2B graphite stick, work into the netting, scribbling in a little more detail.

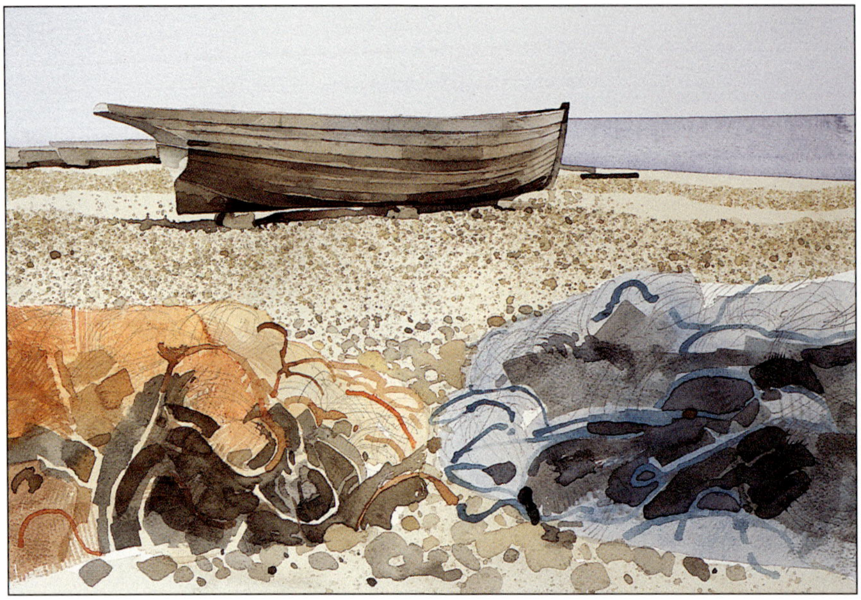

15 The finished picture.

Alternative Approaches

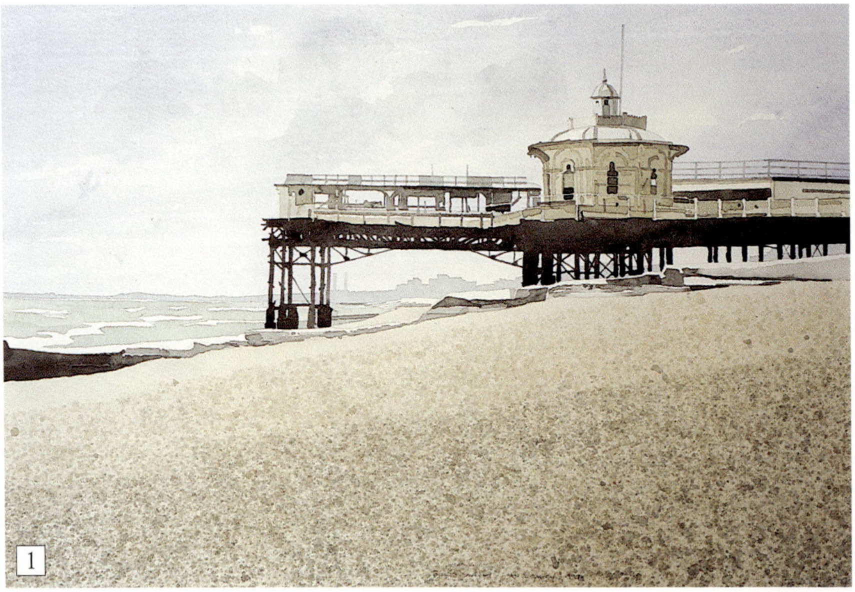

1 The effects of aerial perspective can be clearly seen in this painting of the pier at Brighton, on the south coast of England. The pier itself is painted in sharp, bright colour, while the colour and tone of the distant landscape, glimpsed through the supporting pillars, is muted and cool.

2 A similar effect is achieved, again looking along the beach toward the pier, but from the opposite direction. The muted grey tones of the piers help them to recede into the distance, while the spattering in the foreground, that is suggestive of a pebbled beach, intensifies in colour and increases in size as it nears the foreground or bottom edge of the painting.

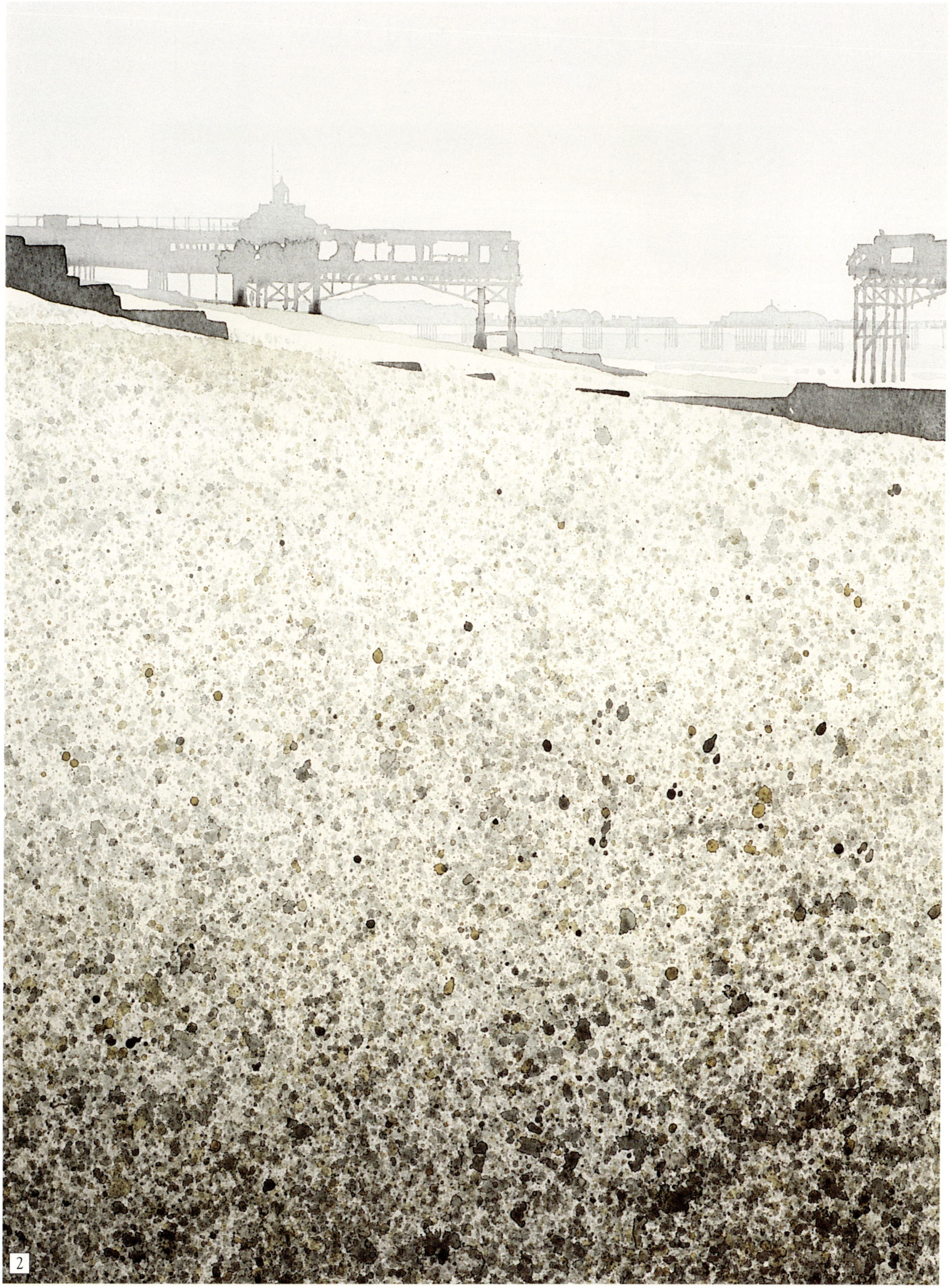

EARLY SNOW

Using White

PROJECT SIX

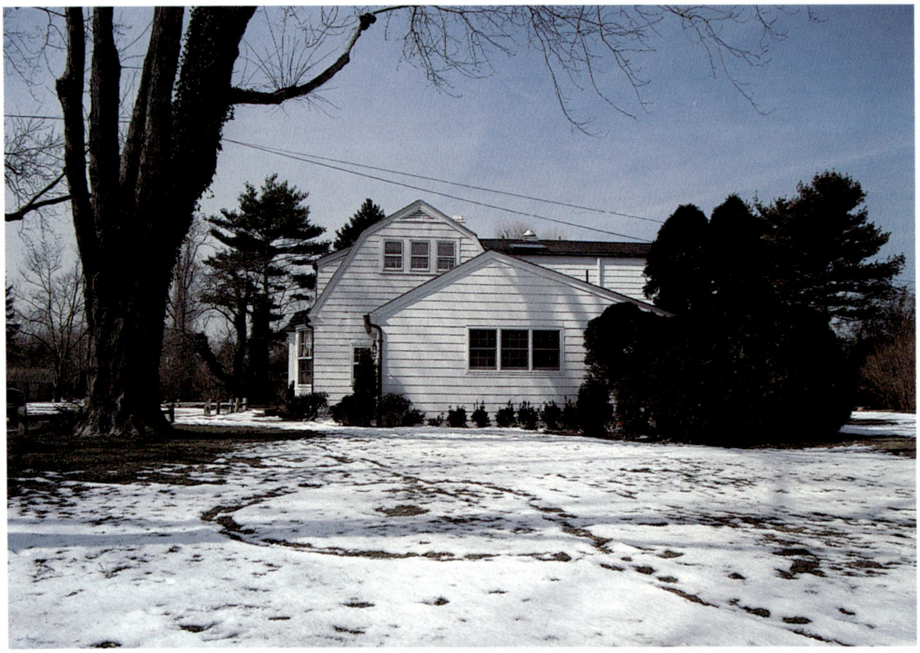

AS STATED previously the white of the support is of primary importance, affecting as it does the intensity and the tone of the colour. A wash with only a little paint added to the water is thinner and allows more light to reflect back from the paper, which in turn makes the colour look paler in tone; darken the mix by adding more pigment to the water and less light can reflect back through the paint, making it look darker in tone. In order to paint something that is white without using white paint, you will need to use the white of the paper. This simply means planning well enough ahead in order to keep that area of paper free of paint. It helps to think in terms of white being a colour and working, as we are, traditionally, that is light to dark: light colours first, dark colours last, so the white colour would come first in the running order.

Once the area that is to be left white has been decided, it can be masked out with paper, tape or masking fluid or carefully avoided and just painted around. How you do this will depend very much on the size and complexity of the white area. If the area consists of thin white lines against a dark background, then it would make sense to use masking fluid for the lines and wash the dark colour over the top. If the white area is a larger, simpler shape then painting around it should present no problems – it may be that a combination of techniques is employed, as we have done here.

The shape of the building was easily avoided with paint, but the grass showing through the snow was a different matter and would have been difficult to show by simply painting the grass around the patches of snow. The problem was solved by using candle wax as a resist on the foreground to keep the paint from the paper and allow white to show through in a complex pattern of shapes. Once colour is applied the white areas will gradually be transformed into positive areas, which take on their own form and dimension, occupying specific positions in space rather than being white holes surrounded by coloured paint.

MATERIALS AND EQUIPMENT

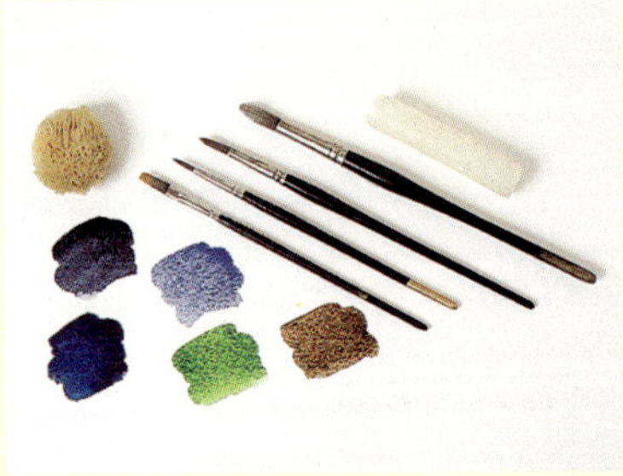

15x22in sheet of stretched 260lb (365gsm) CP Waterford watercolour paper
White candle
Three round brushes, no 12, no 8 and no 5
Small flat brush
Small natural sponge
Watercolours in the following colours: Payne's gray, Antwerp blue, cobalt blue, sap green and raw umber

The Painting

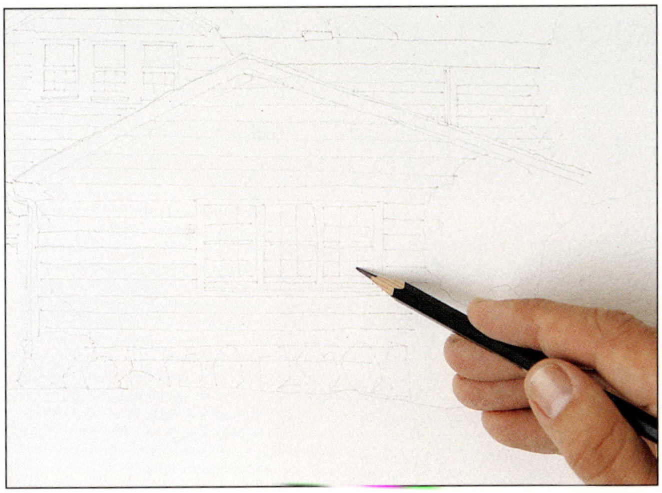

1 It helps to begin with a light line drawing using an HB pencil.

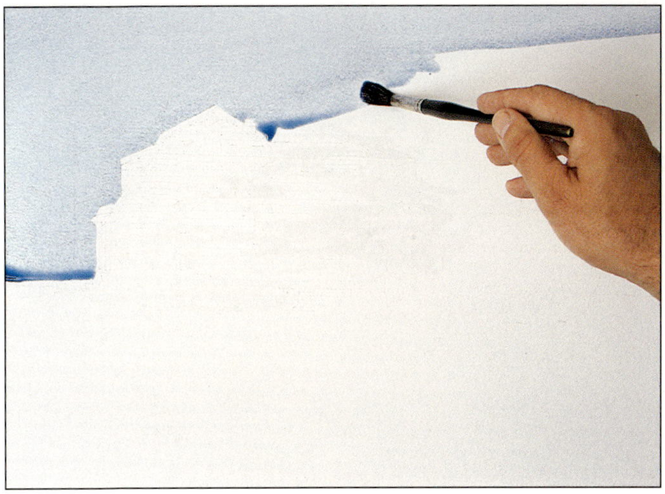

2 Then, using the no 12 round brush, wash in the sky with a light mix consisting of Antwerp and cobalt blue. Allow this to dry.

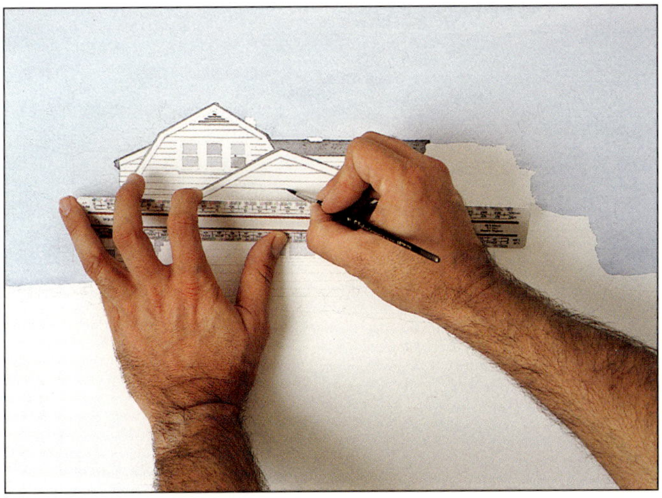

3 With a mix of Payne's gray and raw umber, and using the no 5 round brush, paint in the overall colour of the roof and windows. Then, using a ruler as a guide, paint in the shadow that falls beneath each plank on the house.

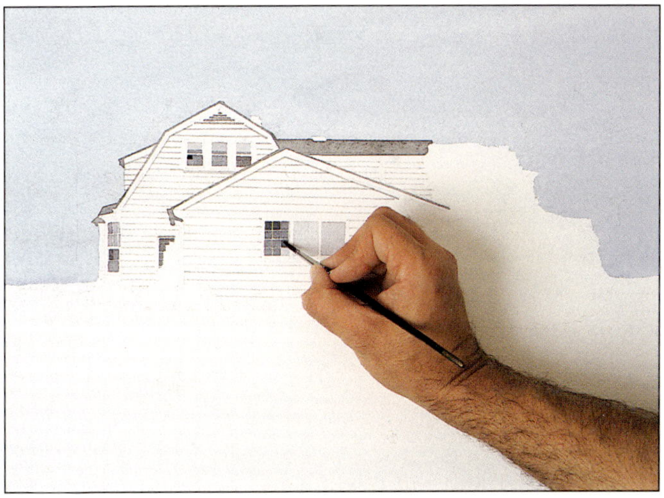

4 Once dry, repaint the individual panes of glass in the windows using the same mix darkened a little with Payne's gray and cobalt blue and also wash in the trees seen in the distance.

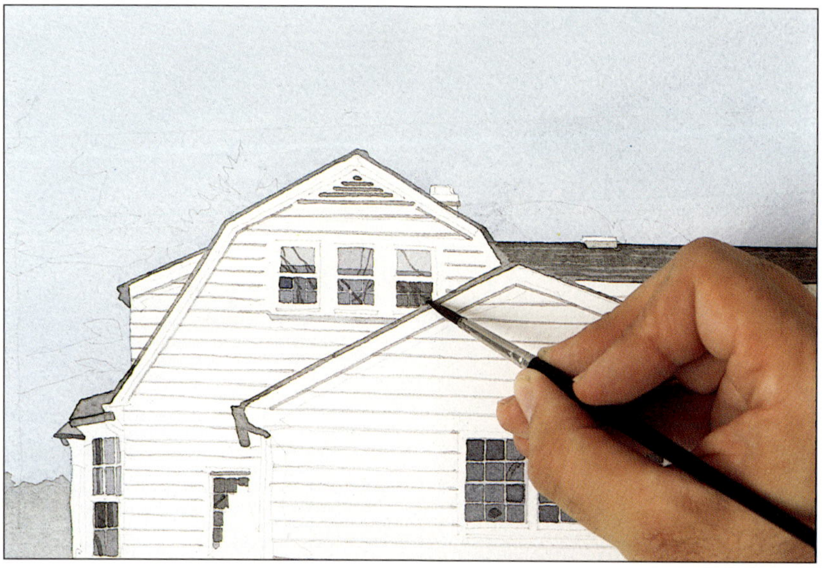

5 Paint in the lines of the roof shingles, darken the mix again with the same colours and paint in the reflection of the tree branches.

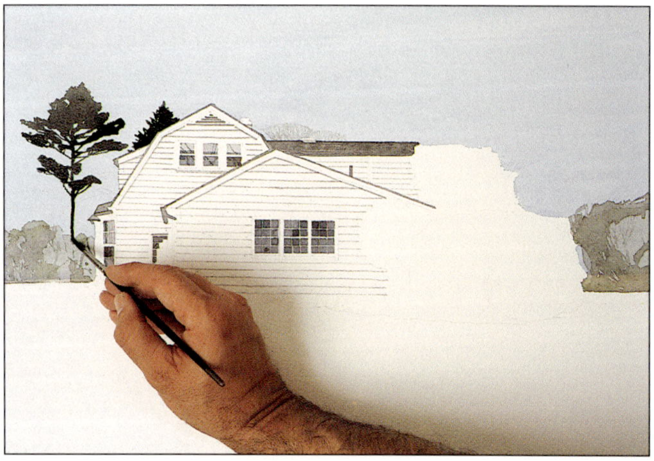

6 Still using the no 5 round brush and with a mix of raw umber and Payne's gray, paint in the branches of the distant trees, which can be seen behind and to the side of the building.

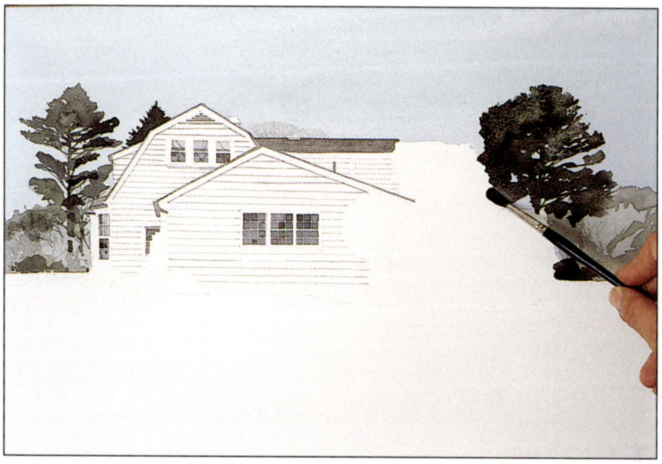

7 Add a little sap green into the previous mix and add more detail to the band of undergrowth that runs across the centre of the picture. Allow this to dry, then rework, painting in a suggestion of trees and branches. Add more sap green and paint in a little foliage, then darken the mix considerably with the addition of more sap green, Payne's gray and raw umber, and using the no 5 and the no 8 round brushes, carefully position the dark trees. Pay particular attention to their shape; do not make them too dense and leave plenty of sky holes.

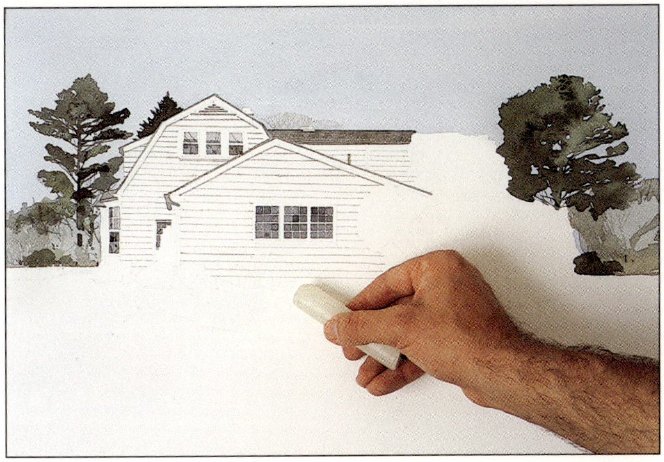

8 Work across the foreground of the painting with the white candle. The wax will act as a resist, repelling the paint and allowing the white of the paper to show through.

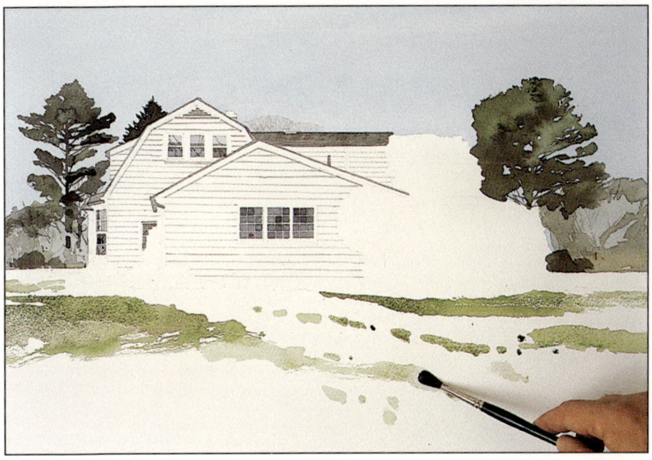

9 Mix sap green, a little Payne's gray and raw umber and, using the no 12 round brush, loosely brush in the grass showing through the light covering of snow.

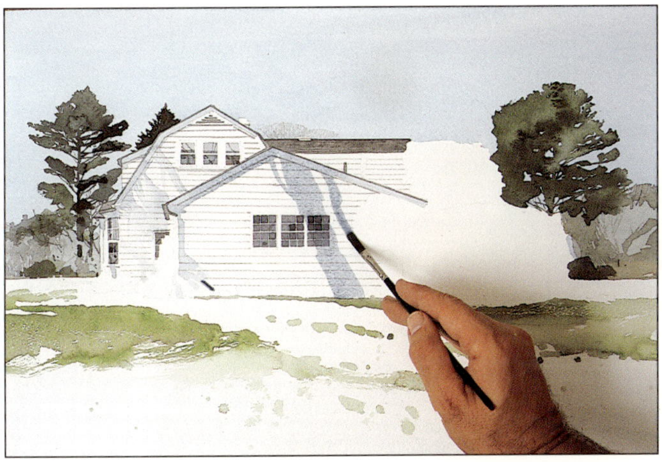

10 Cobalt blue, Antwerp blue and a little Payne's gray give the blue shadow cast by the trees standing just out of view. Using the small flat brush the shadows are painted in simple shapes that run down the white-painted timber and across the windows. The same blue mix is also pulled across the snow and grass, indicating the direction of the shadows that fall there.

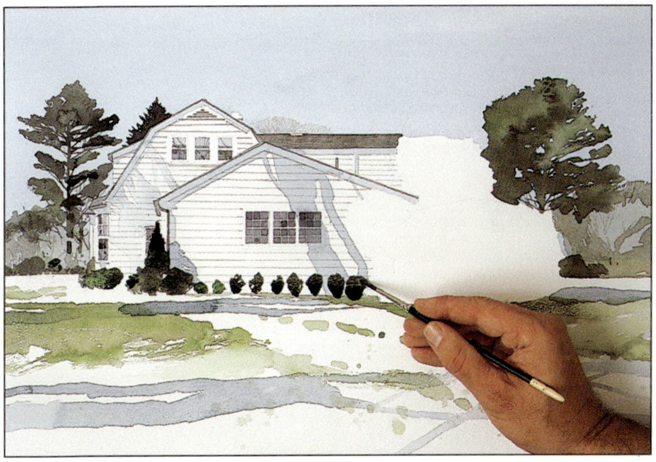

11 Sap green, Payne's gray and raw umber are mixed to give a dark green. Using the no 5 round brush, establish the small shrubs and bushes that are planted around the base of the building.

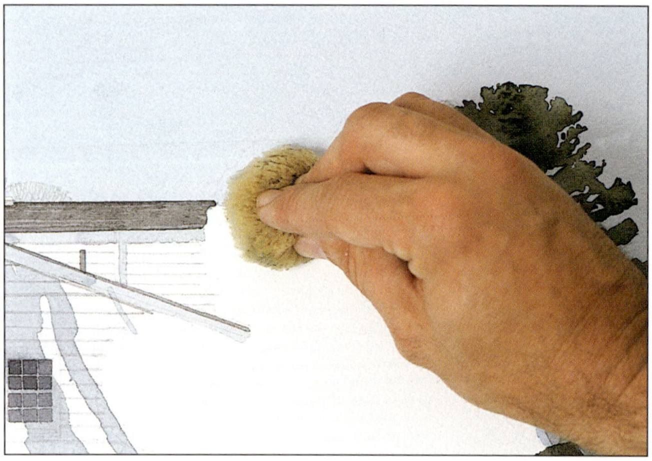

12 The collection of dark shrubs and small trees that stand to one side, but in front of the building, are painted next. In order to give the outline a distinct quality the area is first dabbed with a small, wet natural sponge.

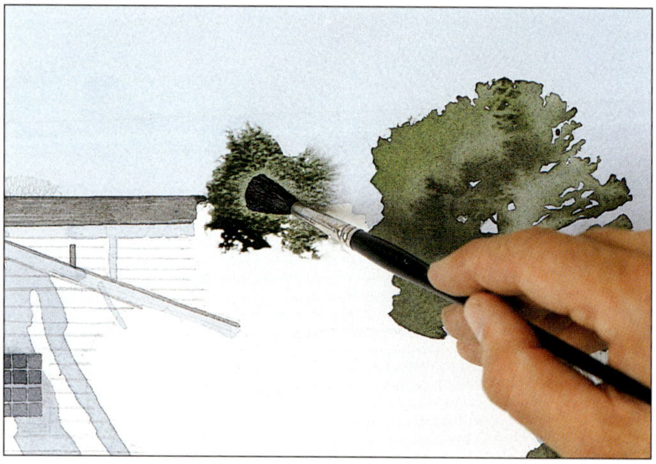

13 Then, using the dark green mix and the no 12 round brush, drop the paint into the area. There is no need to brush the paint into the outline, it will find its own way as it flows into the wet shape left by the sponge.

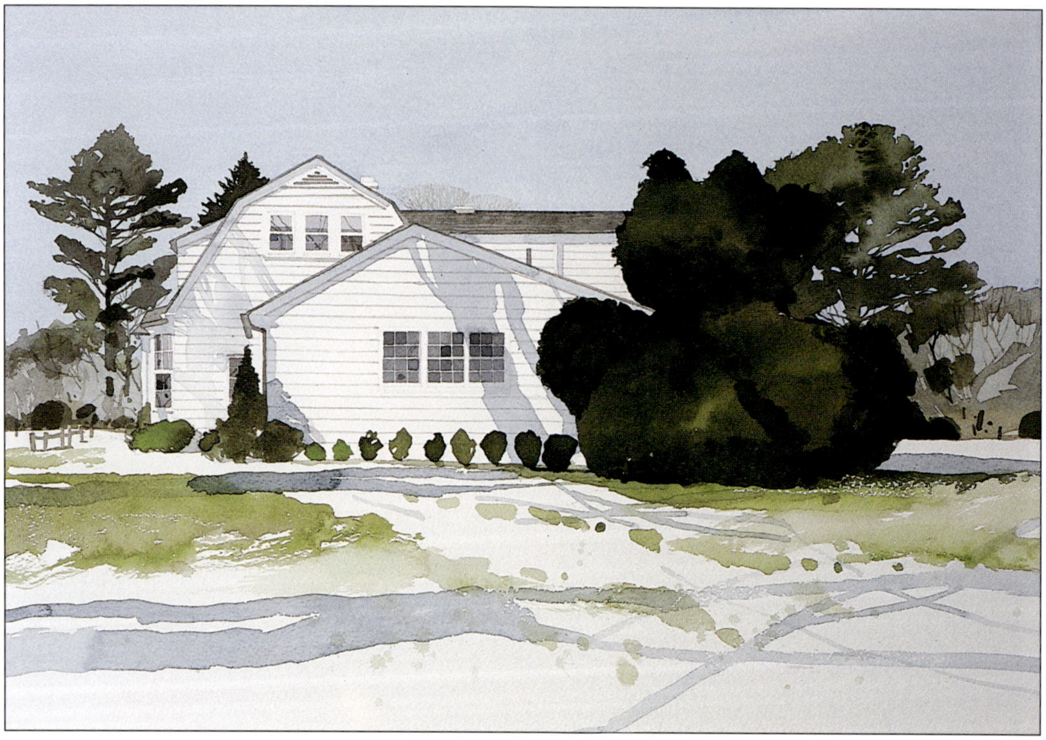

14 The shrubs are darkened a little on the side away from the sun by adding Payne's gray to the dark green mix and the dark shadow cast by a tree that is out of view is painted falling across them with the no 12 round brush and the same mix.

Alternative Approaches

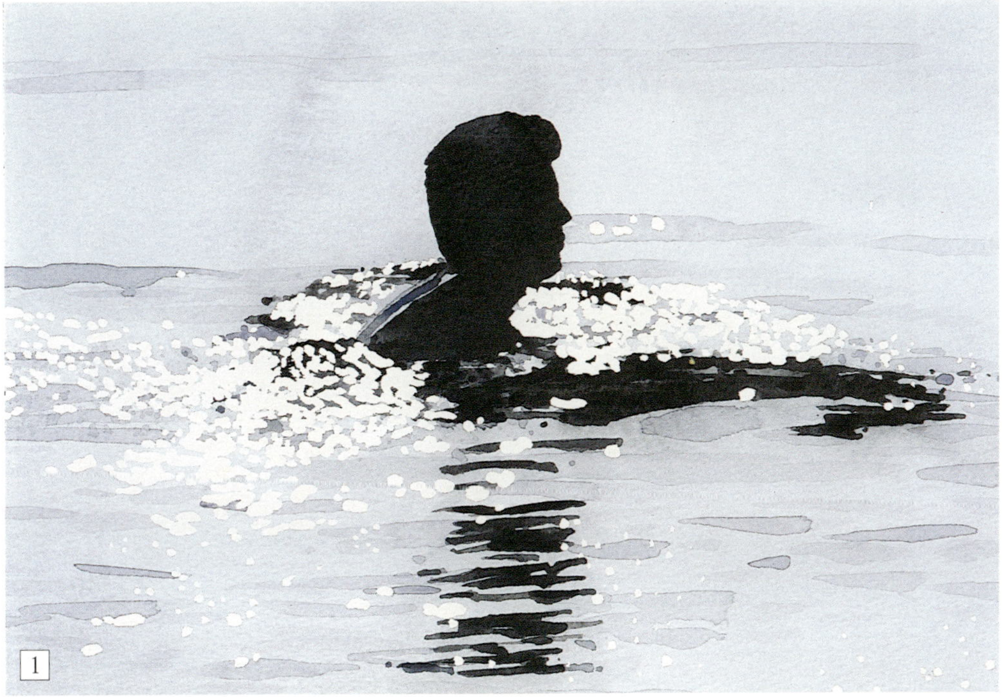

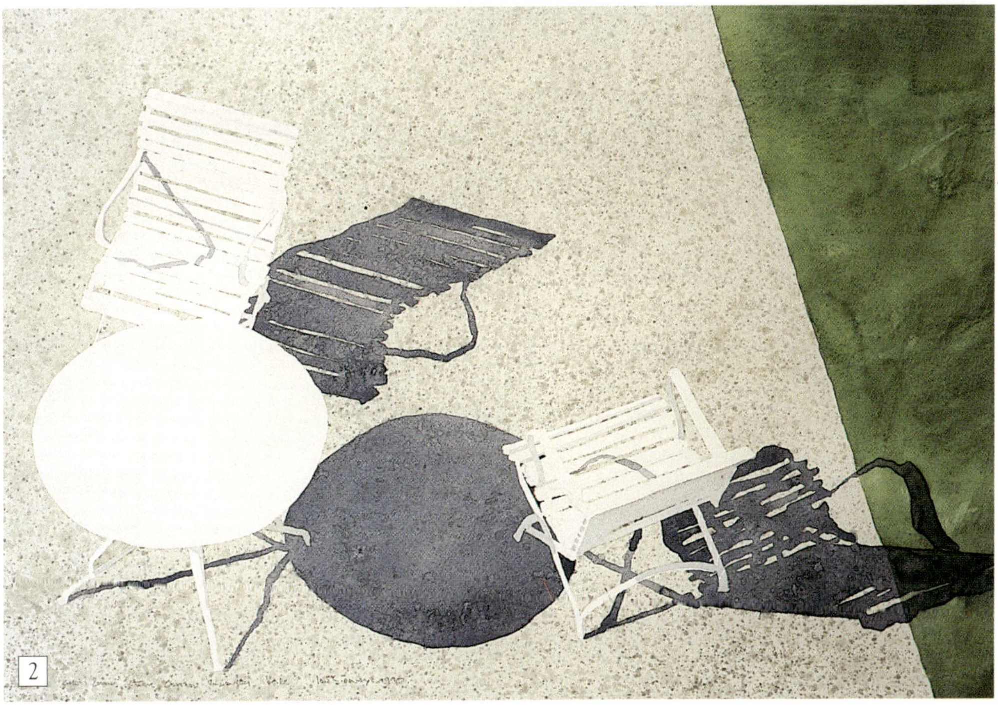

1 In this simple study of a swimmer, only two colours were used. The effect of the sun sparkling on the surface of the water was obtained by dotting on blobs of masking fluid before applying any paint.

2 For this slightly unusual view of a white table and two chairs seen from above, masking fluid was used again to paint the shapes out carefully before commencing work on the loosely painted and spattered background.

ACROSS THE GRAND CANAL

Editing the Scene

PROJECT SEVEN

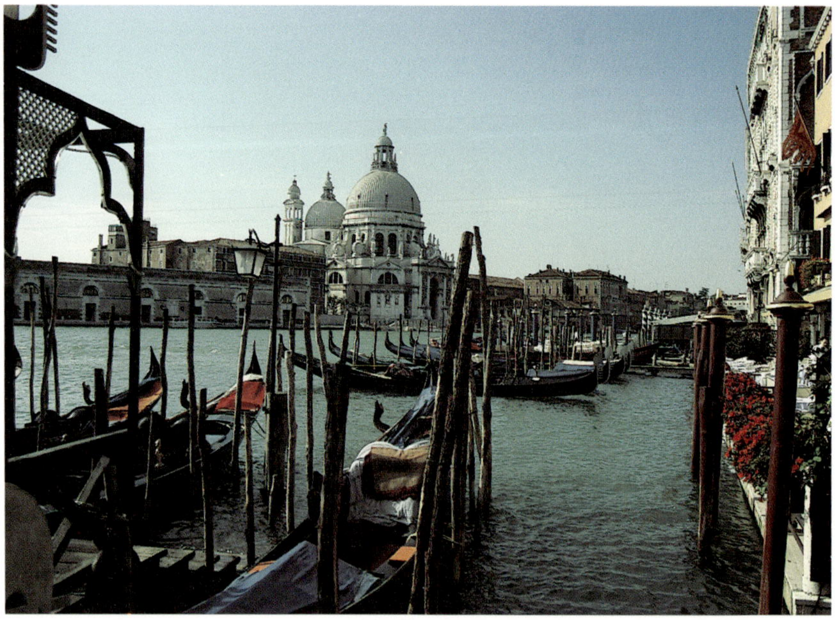

OCCASIONALLY a scene before you looks so complicated it actually puts you off making any attempt to paint it. The answer is not to give up, but to visually edit the scene, leaving out anything that you feel is not needed, simplifying and distilling the view until it appears manageable. One technique that can be helpful is to half-close your eyes and look carefully at the scene. This technique has the effect of reducing the apparent tonal range of the colours and increasing the contrast. It also has the effect of reducing the amount of detail and texture, which is inevitably contributing to the confusion.

This scene across the grand canal in Venice, looking toward Santa Maria della Salute, is a riot of shapes, colours and textures, all screaming for attention. However, it could quite easily be broken down into half a dozen different compositions. Choosing what format and composition to go with are usually two of the early decisions to be made. A number of different compositions and formats can be considered before starting work by using a view finder. You can make one from a small piece of card by cutting a rectangle in the middle. Hold this up in front of you and look through it toward the subject.

Certain elements, as long as they are not too important, can always be left out and others added, as we have done here. It was thought that an extra wooden stake should be added to fill the gap in the lower right hand corner, helping to balance the composition. It may be interesting to note that the well-known 18th century Venetian artist Canaletto sometimes moved entire buildings if they did not suit the scheme of his famous compositions.

The process was further simplified by splitting the picture up into specific areas and methodically working over each in turn; this gives you about as much control as it is possible to have when using watercolours. Most of the colours have been split into just three tones: light, medium and dark. These are worked light first, dark last, and each is allowed to dry before applying the next. But despite this you will see that the tonal range in the painting appears to be much greater.

Materials and Equipment

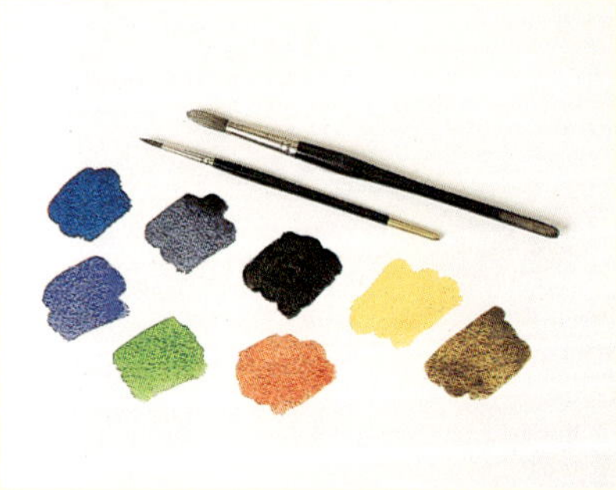

20x14in sheet of stretched 200lb (425gsm) CP Bockingford watercolour paper
Two round brushes, no 12 and no 5
Watercolours in the following colours: Antwerp blue, cobalt blue, Payne's gray, sap green, ivory black, brown madder alizarin, yellow ochre and raw umber

The Painting

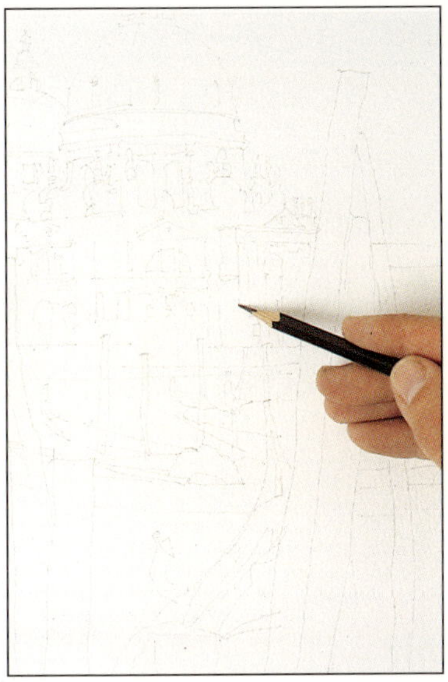

1 With such a complex scene, which requires colour washes to be kept well under control, a light pencil drawing, using an HB pencil, will act as an invaluable guide.

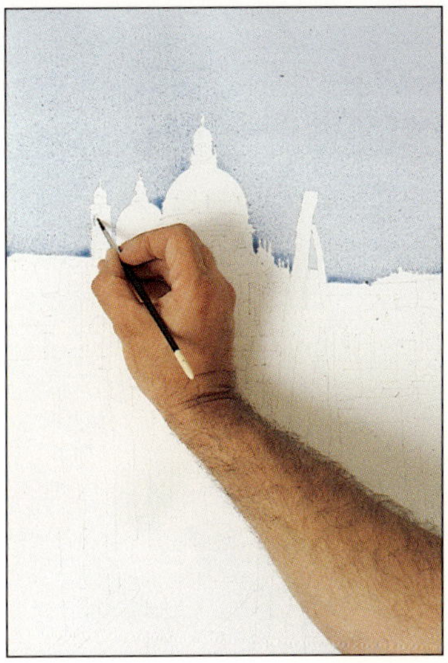

2 Mix up a wash of Antwerp and cobalt blue and, using the no 12 round brush, paint in the sky as a flat wash. Position the board at a slight angle and work quickly, painting as close to the buildings as you can with the large brush. Switch to the smaller no 5 round brush to paint in and around any complicated edges.

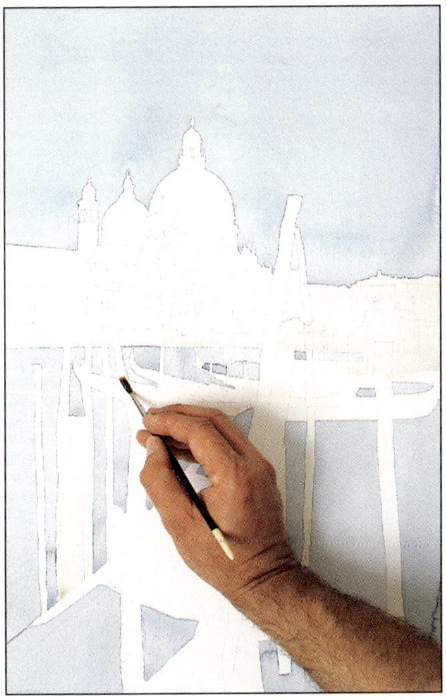

3 Using the same mix, block in the blue canvas covers on the boats and the water, working carefully around the boats and the palina, or wooden stakes, that are used for mooring.

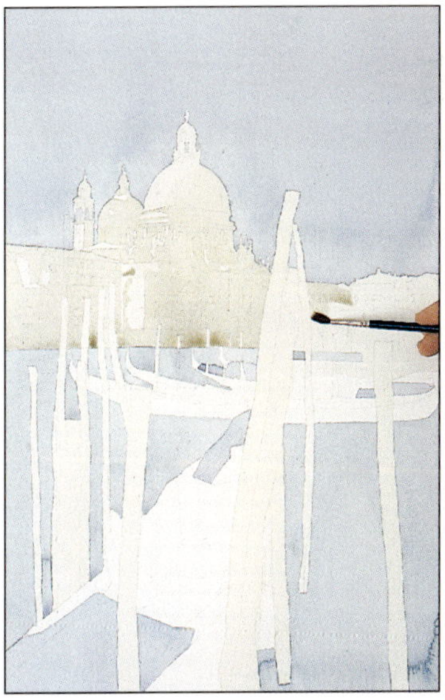

4 Once the blue has thoroughly dried, paint a very pale wash made with yellow ochre and ivory black across the buildings and the wooden stakes. Allow this to dry, then darken and intensify the mix by adding more ochre and black, and apply a second tone across the buildings, this time leaving any light areas and the stakes unpainted. Allow the painting to dry.

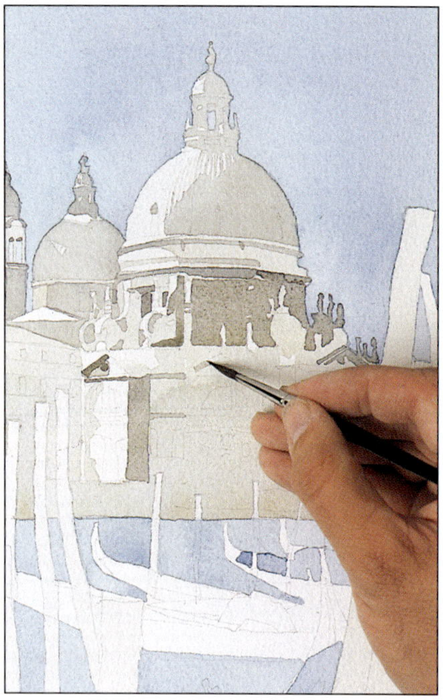

5 Darken the mix once more with ochre and black and carefully and selectively begin to paint in the darker tones, details and shadows seen on the church.

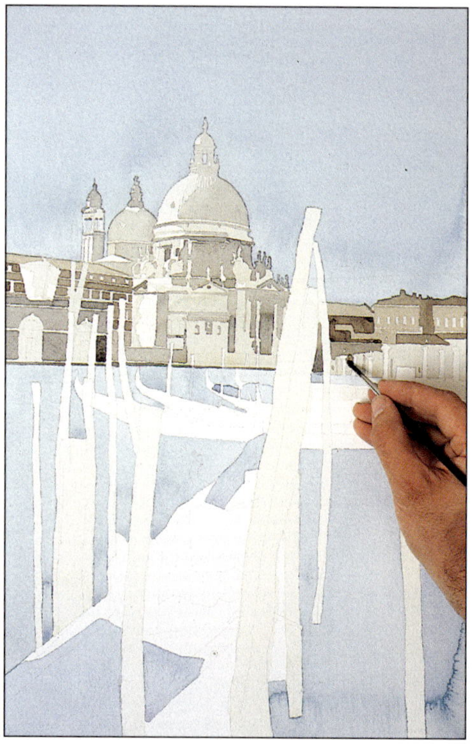

6 Add burnt umber to the mix, making it richer and browner, and in the same way work the buildings either side of the church. Paint in the dark line that runs across the scene at the waters edge.

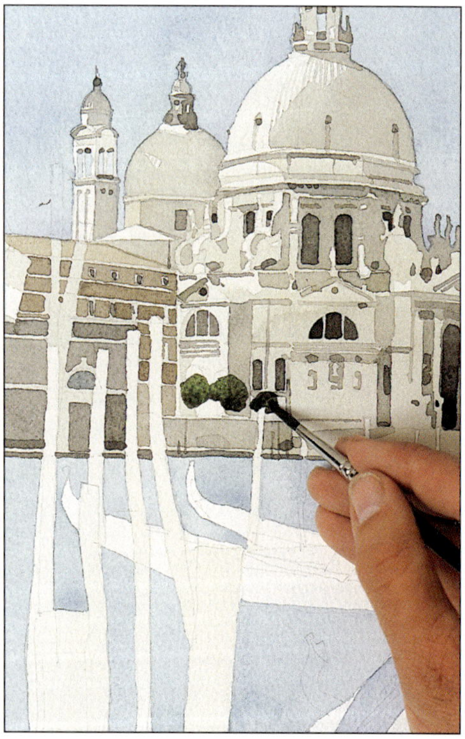

7 Using a still darker mix of raw umber and ivory black, paint the details and shadows seen on the church and the other buildings, paying particular attention to windows and doors. With a sap green and raw umber mix establish the few small trees that stand at the base of the church.

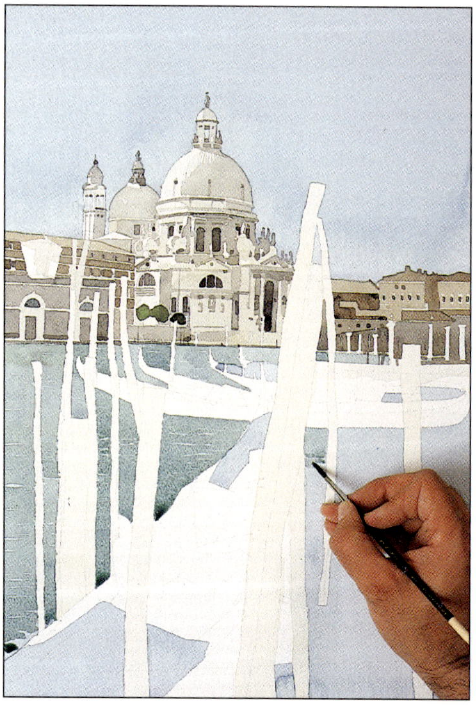

8 Still using the no 5 round brush, mix Antwerp blue, sap green and a little Payne's gray to deaden the colour work across the water, leaving the shape of ripples and small waves showing in places.

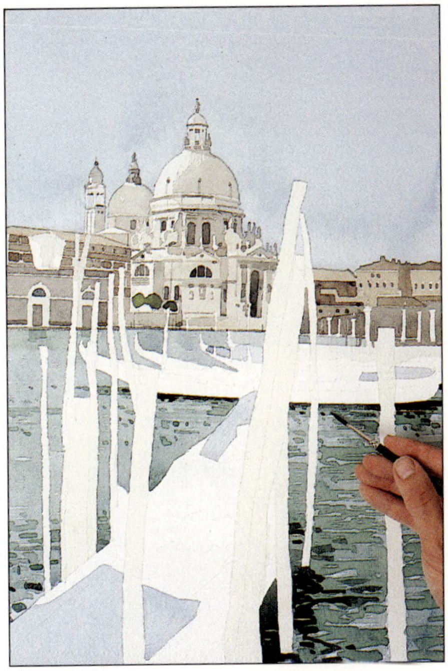

9 Once this is dry, darken the mix with a little Payne's gray and repaint the water, working the shapes seen in the rippled surface. Darken the mix further by adding Payne's gray and paint in the dark shadows and reflections seen beneath the gondolas. Note that by making the ripples larger they appear closer, which helps give the illusion of depth.

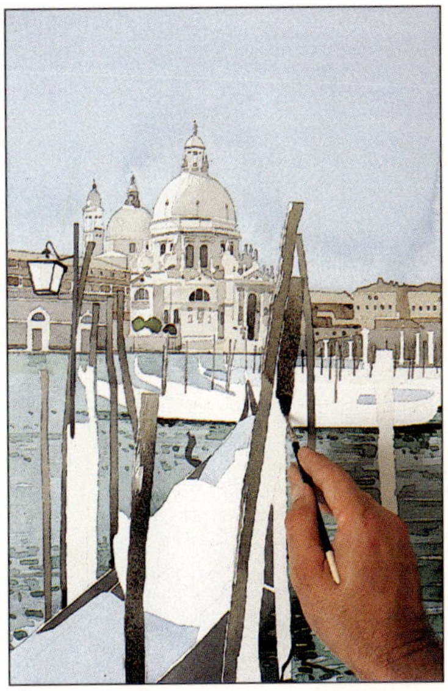

10 Turn your attention to the wooden stakes and block them in with a mixture of raw umber and burnt umber. Leave a little bark texture showing where it catches the light and lighten the mix a little by adding water for those stakes that are situated in the middle distance.

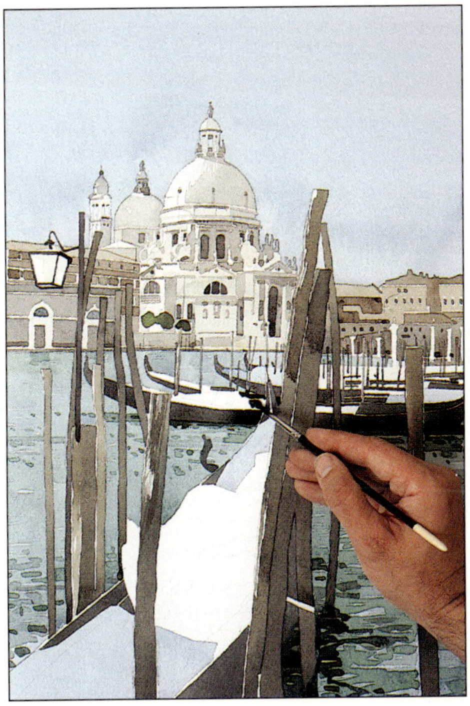

11 Adding ivory black into the mix gives the colour for the gondolas; work carefully around the stakes.

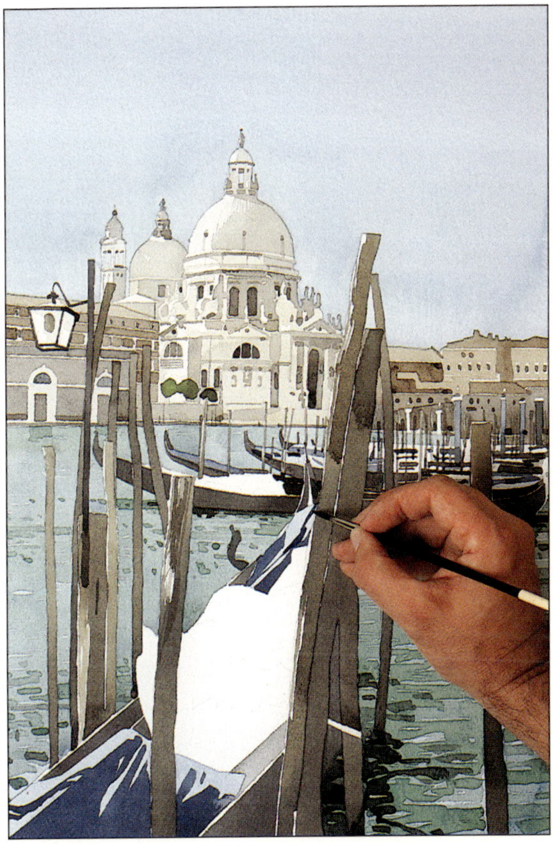

12 With a dark blue mixed from Payne's gray and Antwerp blue, paint in the shadows seen on the blue canvas covers.

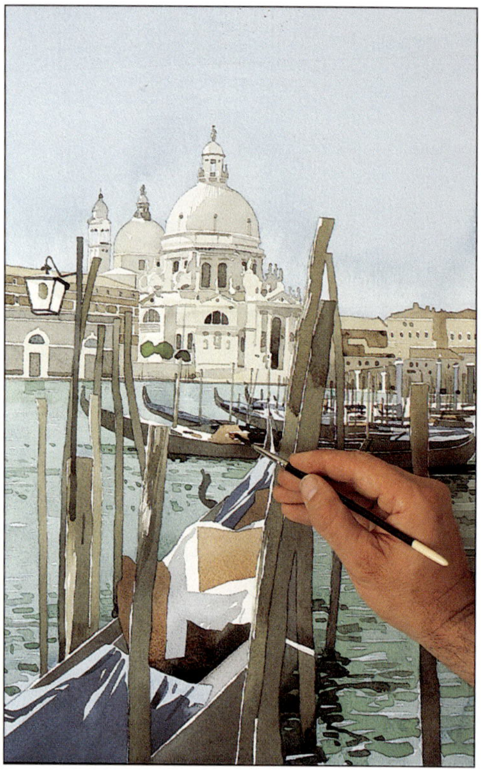

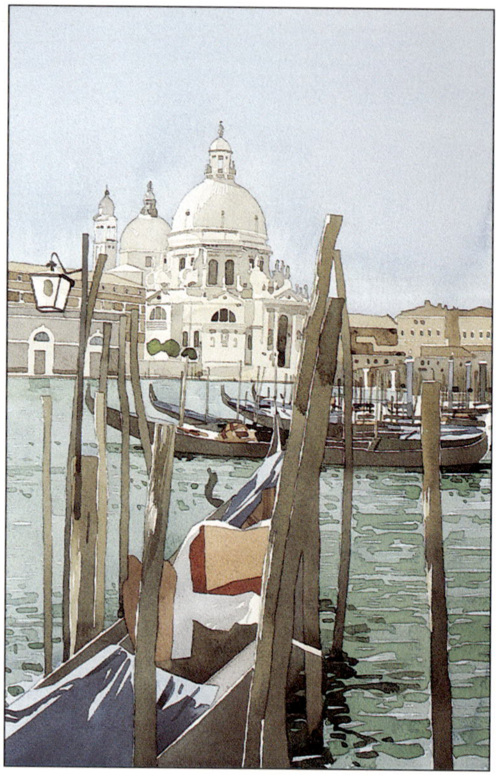

13 Payne's gray and ivory black give a light grey for the shadow on the cover in the nearest boat, while brown madder alizarin and raw umber give a dull, washed out red for the other covers and blankets.

14 Finally, add more brown madder alizarin to redden the mix and paint in the pattern seen on the blankets and the dark red surround on the seat cover of the nearest boat.

Alternative Approaches

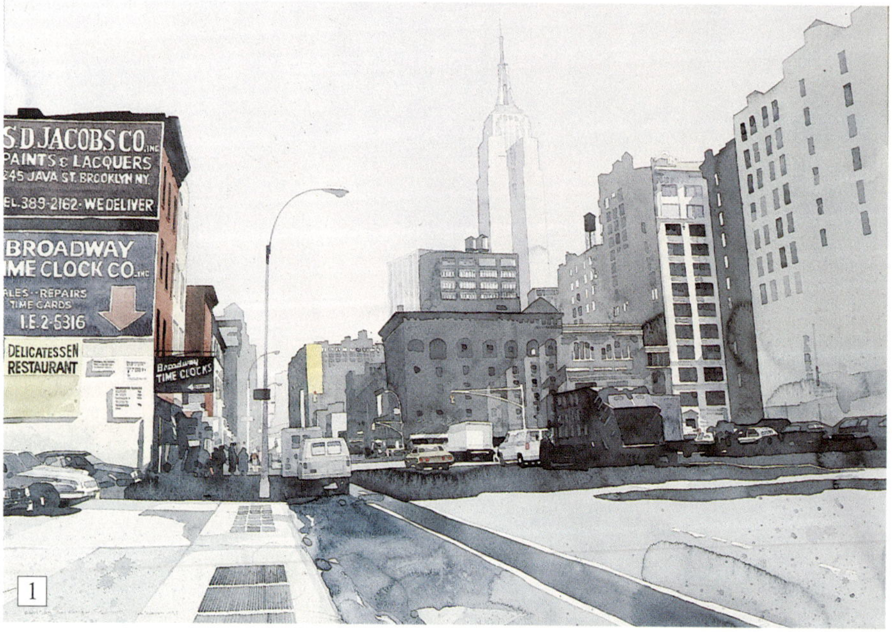

1

1 This large painting looking up Seventh Avenue in New York is painted with very few colours. Varying mixes, using Payne's gray and ivory black, are enlivened by a little colour on the buildings to the left, and the red touches seen in the brake and traffic lights.

2 In this painting, looking out of a window in the Louvre, Paris, the tonal contrasts are pushed to the extreme, with the building opposite painted in cool, light tones giving a sense of distance and the window frame and tree painted very dark, almost black.

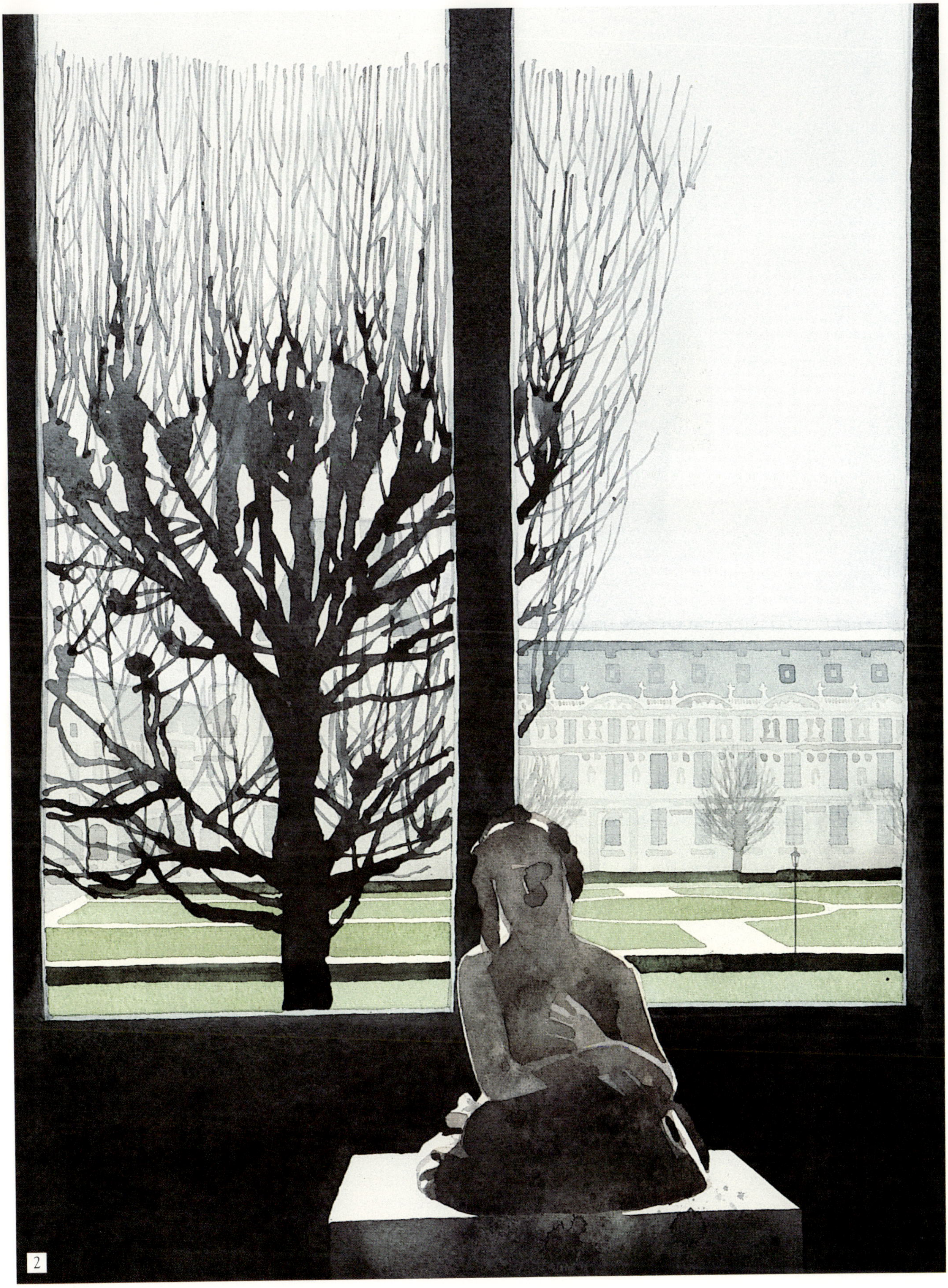

2

ALICE

Controlling Washes and Making Corrections

PROJECT EIGHT

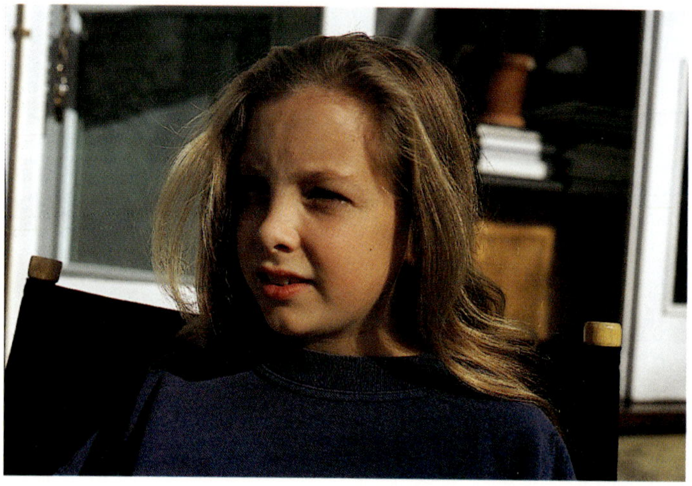

MANY WILL AGREE, I am sure, that portraits are perhaps the most difficult thing to paint convincingly. It is quite enough having to juggle with the complexities of proportion, form, colour and tone, not to mention composition, without the added challenge of trying to capture something of the sitter's character and personality. Children can be particularly demanding, as their attention span is short and they have great difficulty in sitting still for any period of time. Working from photographs is an obvious solution, relieving the tension that both the artist and young model would have inevitably felt, and enabling the artist to take a longer, more considered approach. Photographic reference can be unhelpful though – the main problem lies in the camera's monocular viewpoint of seeing things, as it does, from only one point in space. The binocular vision that humans possess gives a three-dimensional viewpoint; even a very small movement of the head will alter the angle at which the subject is seen, making it possible to assess form, shape and colour more easily. However, that said, these problems can be overcome if the photographic reference is used correctly and with a little thought.

With opaque mediums such as oil or acrylic paint alterations and corrections are easily effected simply by painting over and obliterating what was there beneath a new layer of paint. As we have already seen, there is no such luxury with watercolour, so working on a portrait, with its subtle variations in skin tone and colour, will test your mixing, as well as your light to dark wash techniques, to the full. Always remember it is easier to darken an area or wash than it is to lighten one; a great deal of gum arabic was used in the middle and later stages of this portrait painting for precisely that reason. It enabled paint to be rewet and lifted, and hard edges softened; it also kept the colour bright and transparent.

Obtaining a likeness is often simply a matter of widening the mouth, lengthening the nose or altering the curve of the cheek, and you will find that the gum arabic will give you some latitude to enable you to make this kind of alteration. It may seem an odd thing to say, but keep in touch with the progress of the painting from the outset and try to recognise when, and if, things are not right immediately.

While it may be somewhat awkward correcting mistakes when a wash is wet, it is impossible when the paint is dry and covered with other washes. Pay particular attention to the intensity of your colour mixes and bear in mind that the colour will look considerably darker when it has dried. To this end, get into the habit of dabbing a little of your mix onto a piece of scrap paper of the same make you are using, and let the colour dry before reassessing its strength.

MATERIALS AND EQUIPMENT

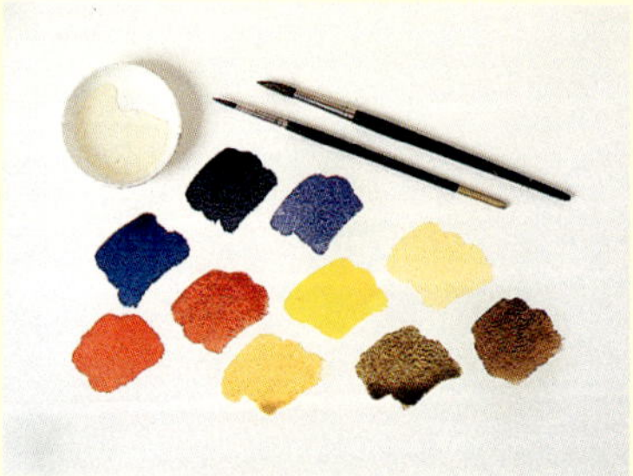

12x10in sheet of unstretched 250lb (535gsm) Bockingford watercolour paper
Two round brushes, no 9 and no 5
Gum arabic
Watercolours in the following colours: Payne's gray, ultramarine, cadmium red, cobalt blue, brown madder alizarin, Naples yellow, yellow ochre, cadmium yellow, raw umber and burnt umber

The Painting

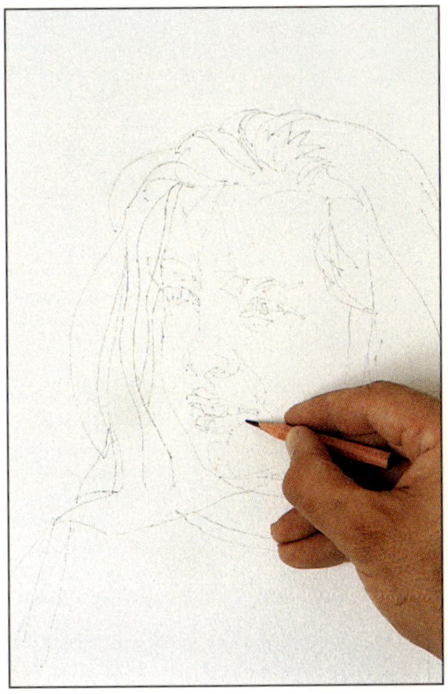

1 Using an HB pencil make a careful line drawing of the subject. Keep the lines light, as they will show through the paint if they are too dark.

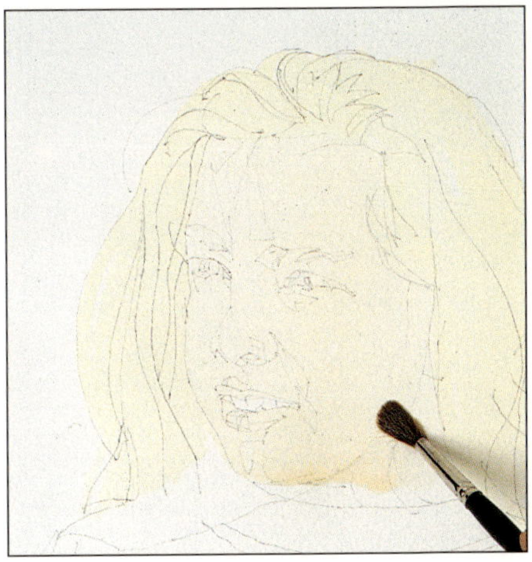

2 Using the no 9 round brush wash in the pale blond hair with a mix of cadmium and Naples yellow. With the same brush, wash in the palest skin tone using a mix of cadmium red and Naples yellow, taking care to work around the white teeth.

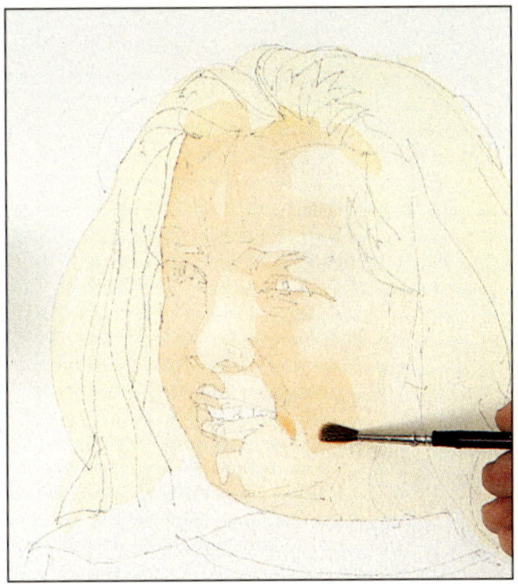

3 Darken the skin mix by adding brown madder alizarin; use the no 5 round brush to work over the face, establishing the mid tone. To avoid getting a hard line, soften the edge of the colour where it ends on the cheek and the forehead by blotting with a paper towel or a barely damp, clean sponge.

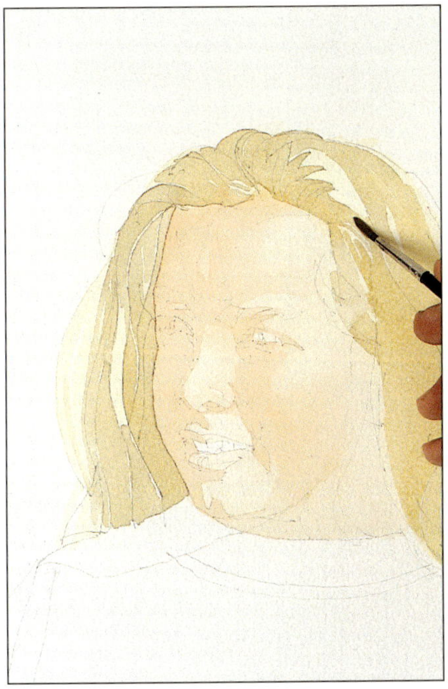

4 Darken the hair mixture with yellow ochre and raw umber and work across the hair, cutting around any highlights.

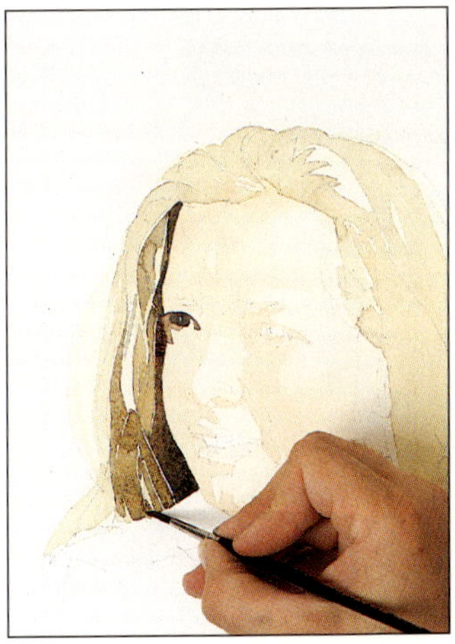

5 With a Payne's gray, raw umber and brown madder alizarin mix paint in the dark of the right eye and the shadow down the side of the face beneath the hair. Darken the hair mix with more yellow ochre and raw umber and search out the shanks and fall of hair, working carefully around any lighter strands.

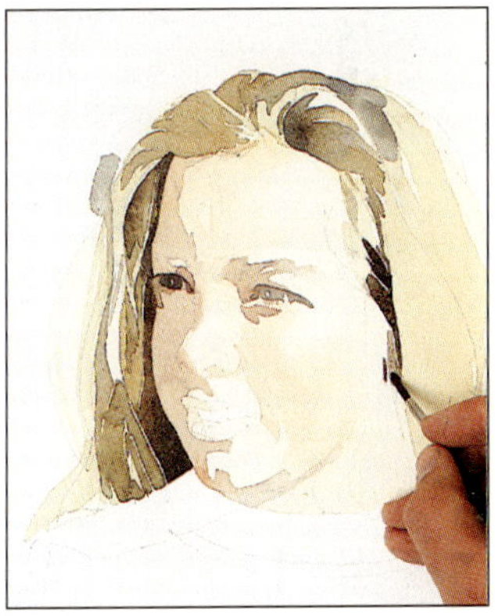

6 Darken the mid skin tone with more brown madder alizarin; add a little cobalt blue and gum arabic and paint in the dark tone on the side of the face and around the left eye. Add water and cobalt blue to show the reflected colour from the blue shirt beneath the chin. Paint in the left eye with Payne's grey and burnt umber and work the dark shadows on the hair.

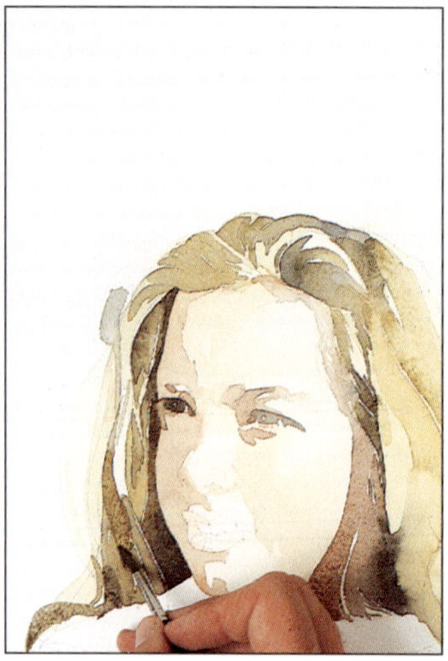

7 Add more brown madder alizarin, cobalt blue and gum arabic into the skin colour and block in the shadow cast by the hair onto the left-hand side of the face. Darken the hair mix further and add a little gum arabic. Using a range of tones rework the hair, darkening and redefining the shapes and shadows.

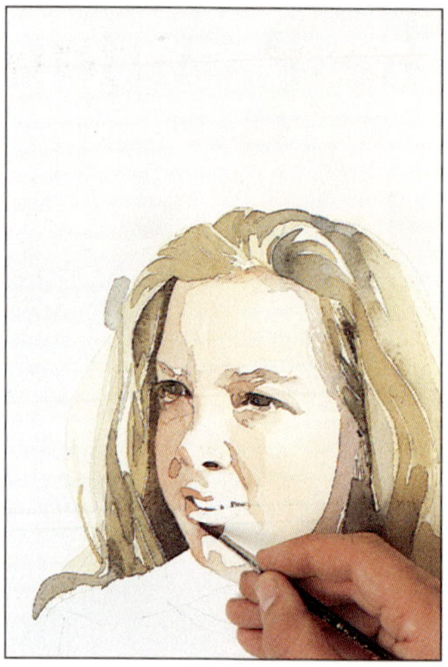

8 Work the subtle tones around the eyes with the skin mix, paint in the shadows at the side and below the nose. With brown madder alizarin and Payne's gray darken the eyes and paint in the nostrils and the dark area inside the mouth. Once this is dry give a little more definition to the eyelids and, using brown madder alizarin, establish the dark on the lips.

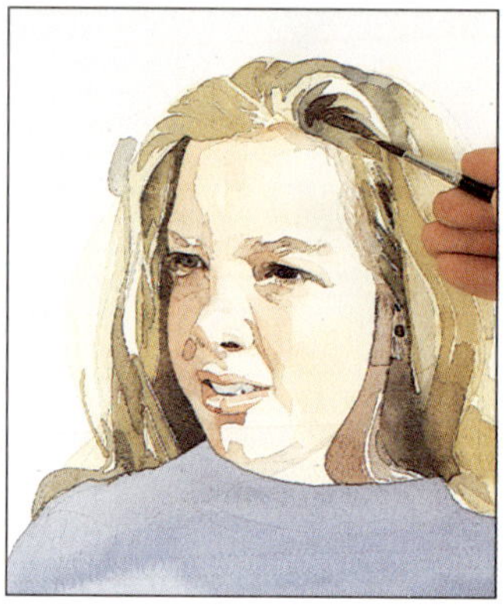

9 An ultramarine and Payne's gray wash establishes the colour of the shirt. To avoid smudging the wet paint allow this to dry, then rework the lips with a range of tones and colours made from brown madder alizarin, cadmium red and cadmium yellow. Mix in gum arabic to sharpen the colour. Allow the lips to dry and paint in the shadow on the teeth with a pale mix of Payne's gray and yellow ochre. Use a dark mix of Payne's gray and burnt umber to darken the iris and pupils, then return to the hair and darken the shadows.

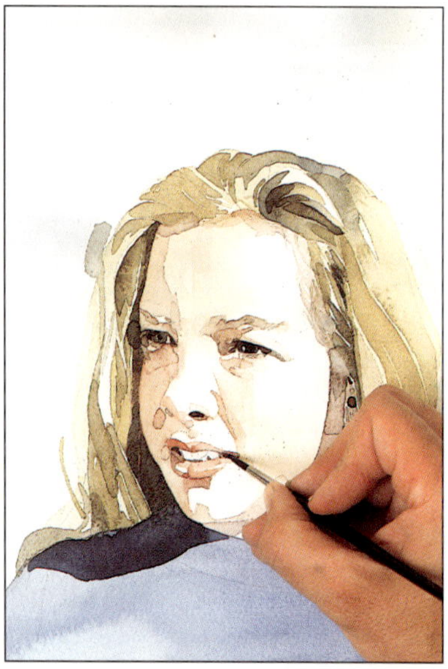

10 Payne's gray mixed with ultramarine is used to paint in the shadow on the sweatshirt. For the shadow on the subjects right lighten the mix with water. Rework the detail on the lips and around the mouth with more lip colour, carefully avoiding the highlights and the teeth.

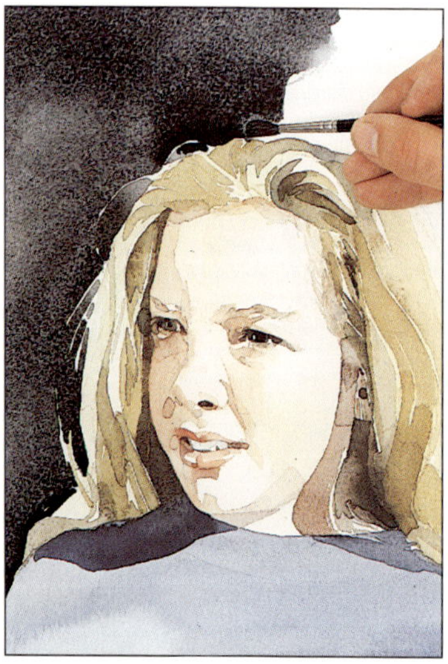

11 Mix a dark wash of burnt umber and Payne's gray and paint in the background using the no 9 round brush. Switch back to the no 5 round brush when painting in close around the hair. Pick out a few wisps of hair by simply leaving thin, curving lines of white paper showing.

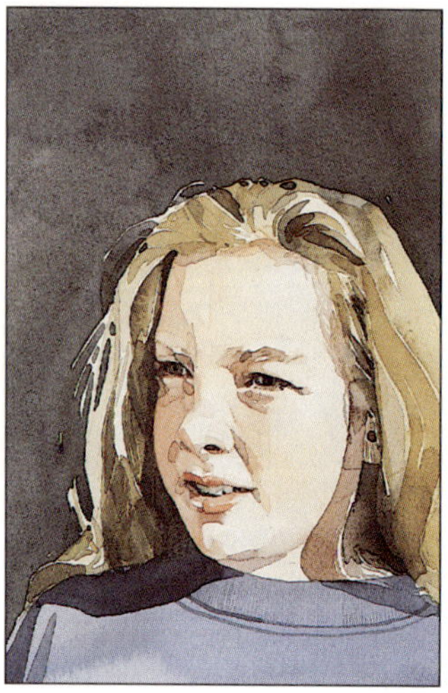

12 Using the no 5 round brush, rework the painting using clean water. The paint, having been mixed with plenty of gum arabic, can be dissolved easily, allowing areas to be softened and manipulated until the result is considered satisfactory.

Alternative Approaches

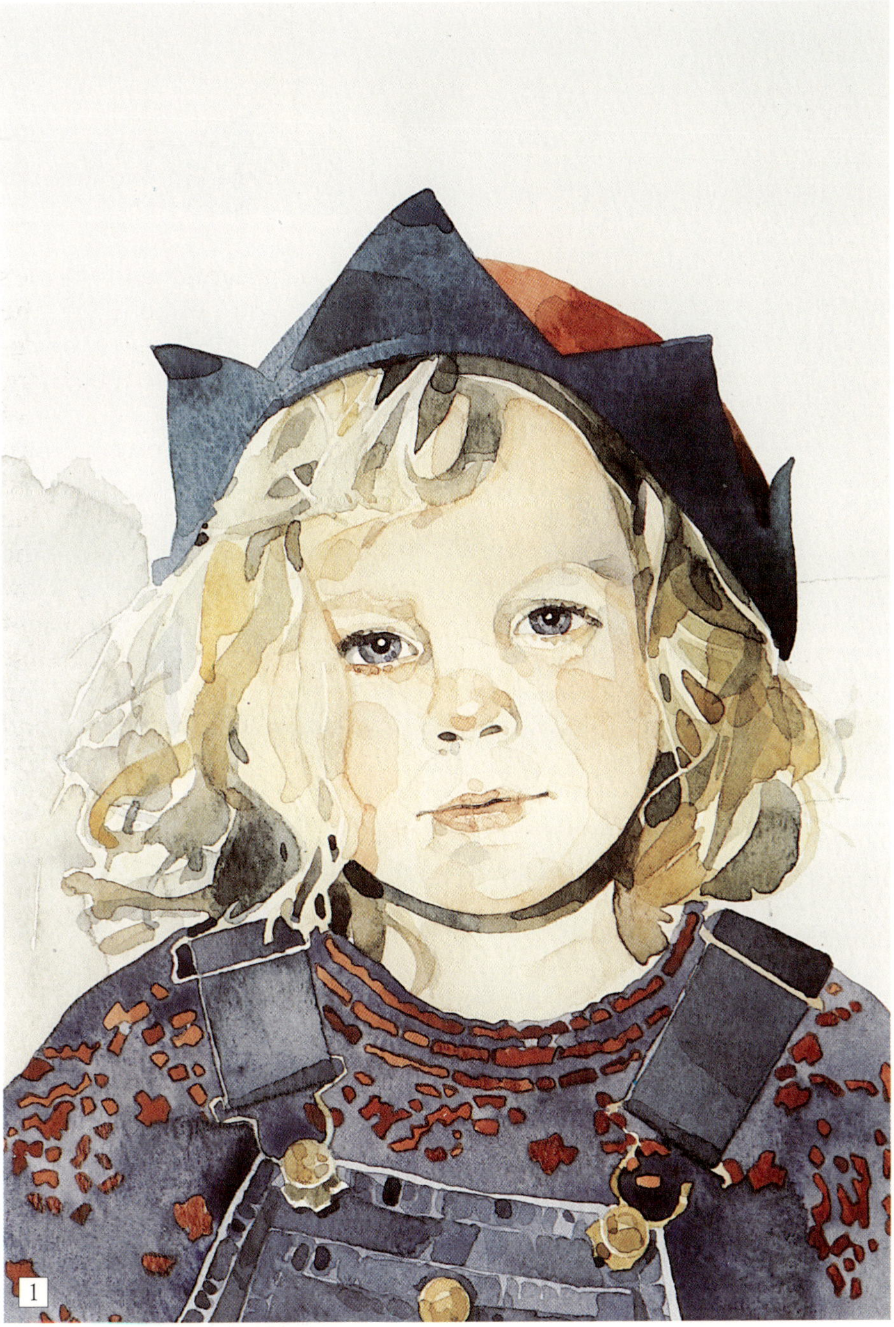

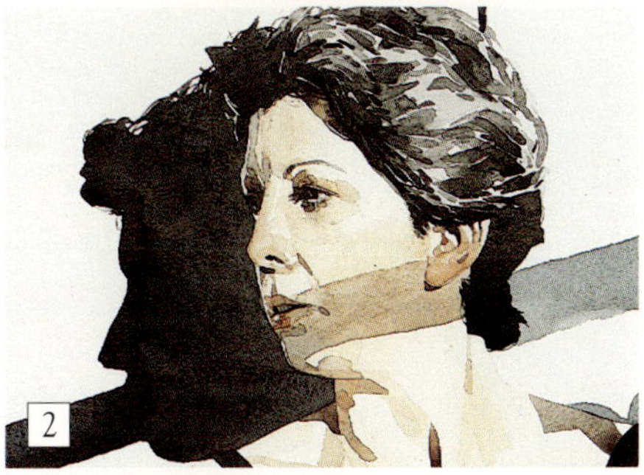

2 The shadow thrown across the sitter's face by the strong light streaming through a window makes a slightly unusual portrait.

1 In this portrait delicate washes – some worked wet into wet, others wet on dry – combine to capture the confident stare of a three-year-old. Portraits painted full on from the front can sometimes look flat, but here the curve of the hat sitting on the back of the head helps give the head dimension.

INDEX